A NEW HEART

Eleven Qualities of Holiness

ROBERT MORNEAU

ORBIS BOOKS

Maryknoll, New York 10545

Founded in 1970, Orbis Books endeavors to publish works that enlighten the mind, nourish the spirit, and challenge the conscience. The publishing arm of the Maryknoll Fathers & Brothers, Orbis seeks to explore the global dimensions of the Christian faith and mission, to invite dialogue with diverse cultures and religious traditions, and to serve the cause of reconciliation and peace. The books published reflect the views of their authors and do not represent the official position of the Maryknoll Society. To learn more about Maryknoll and Orbis Books, please visit our website at www.maryknoll.org.

Library of Congress Cataloging-in-Publication Data

Morneau, Robert F., 1938-
  A new heart : eleven qualities of holiness / Robert Morneau.
     p. cm.
  ISBN-13: 978-1-57075-801-0 (pbk.)
  1. Christian life—Catholic authors. 2. Holiness—Catholic
Church—Meditations. I. Title.
  BX2350.3.M66 2008
  248.4—dc22
                                         2008016329

CONTENTS

PREFACE

Ezekiel the prophet is a messenger of hope. In the following passage, he communicates God's promise, a promise that is revolutionary and radical. If we put our trust in God's word, we will become a new creation.

> For I will take you away from among the foreign lands, and bring you back to your own land. I will sprinkle clean water upon you to cleanse you from all your impurities, and from all your idols I will cleanse you. I will give you a new heart and place a new spirit within you, taking from your bodies your stony hearts and giving you natural hearts. I will put my spirit within you and make you live by my statutes, careful to observe my decrees. (Ezekiel 36:24–27)

That promise took on greater specificity when I read a prayer composed by Dag Hammarskjold (1905–1961) in his personal journal, *Markings*. The former secretary general of the United Nations asked God for a heart containing four qualities: purity, humility, love, and faith:

> Give me a pure heart—that I may see Thee,
> a humble heart—that I may hear Thee,
> a heart of love—that I may serve Thee,
> a heart of faith—that I may abide in Thee.

Over the years I have often recited this prayer, desiring, like Hammarskjold, an inner transformation. As the years moved on, my desire expanded as I realized the need for other qualities as well. To the four requests found in *Markings*, I added seven more: courage, joy, praise, gratitude, kindness, hospitality, and hope:

Give me a heart of courage, that I may follow Thee,
a heart of joy, that I may sing with Thee,
a heart of praise, that I may adore Thee,
a heart of gratitude, that I may thank Thee,
a heart of kindness, that I may emulate Thee,
a heart of hospitality, that I may welcome Thee,
a heart of hope, that I may trust in Thee.

The following reflections flesh out these desires. From life experiences, poetry, and other sources, I have attempted to articulate the meanings and implications of being gifted with a new heart. More, I have attempted to transform the prayer into concrete actions, failing more often than succeeding. Yet there is a consolation. Human effort, though significant, pales before the Lord's promise: "I will give you a new heart." Indeed, this is the promise that keeps us from discouragement.

WEEK ONE

A Pure Heart
That I May See Thee!

A SAINT

A third grader got it right.
"A saint is someone that
the light shines through."

She was looking at a stained glass window—
the one St. Francis inhabits.
Every morning the light comes
and Francis lets the light pass through.

Saint are bearers of the light
and love
and life.

Just ask any third grader.

Purity has something to do with luminosity. One experience of purity came while leaning over the side of a boat
and being able to see clear to the bottom of the lake. The
water was fresh and clean, unpolluted by industrial waste
or anything else. It was a "pure" moment, with nothing
there to inhibit the light. Luminous was that moment!
Like St. Francis in the window and in life, the light pro-
vided a marvelous transparency.

Another awareness of what purity might be came at a concert. The trumpeter stood before the audience, lifted his horn, and filled the concert hall with such clarity of sound that the only word I could find to describe the moment was "pure." It was as if the melody and tonality of that grace embraced all of us into oneness, yes, into a community bonded by a common experience. Each note received its reverence; every bar, its proper weight. Here was a purity that was truly ecstatic.

Though clarity described the tonality, this purity of sound also touched our sight as well as our hearing. We "saw" beauty flowing from the trumpeter's magnificent sound. We "saw" our narrow individuality breaking down as we were drawn up into the intimacy of the moment. It was a beauty uncontaminated by self-interest. It was a "holy" moment, undisturbed by regrets of the past or worries about the future. Purity has the quality of what is called the sacrament of the moment, the sacrament of light.

DAY ONE
All Purity Is One

All sensuality is one, though it takes many forms; all purity is one. It is the same whether a man eat, or drink, or cohabit, or sleep sensually. They are but one appetite, and we only need to see a person do any one of these things to know how great a sensualist he is. The impure can neither stand nor sit with purity.

—Henry David Thoreau

REFLECTION

In his autobiographical work *Report to Greco*, Nikos Kazantzakis relates his life-long struggle with his double inheritance. From his mother he felt the call to holiness; from his father, a deeply embedded sensuality. Most of us can identify with this warfare between our physical and spiritual desires. And, just as holiness is essentially singular in nature, so too is the sensual side of our nature. It's all of a piece, whether we are dealing with food or drink, sleep or sexuality. Close observation of any one of these in our lives reveals every other dimension. Thus, those who wish to conceal any area of life must be constantly on guard, since we continually give ourselves away.

ACTION

Whenever impurities of mind, body, imagination, or memory arise, gently make the Sign of the Cross over your heart and ask God to have pity on you.

That Triple Purity

*But the path of self-purification is hard and steep. To attain
to perfect purity one has to become absolutely passion-free
in thought, speech and action; to rise above the opposing
currents of love and hatred, attachment and repulsion. I
know that I have not in me as yet that triple purity, in
spite of constant ceaseless striving for it. That is why the
world's praise fails to move me, indeed it very often stings
me. To conquer the subtle passions seems to me to be
harder by far than the physical conquest of the world by
the force of arms. Ever since my return to India I have had
experiences of dormant passions lying hidden within me.*

—Mohandas K. Gandhi

REFLECTION

Often a destructive passion underlies our thoughts,
our words, and our actions. Blind desires drive us
toward unhealthy relationships, incivility in discourse, and cruelty in what we do to others. To
name these "subtle passions" and to conquer them
is a lifelong endeavor. No one is totally successful,
for passions, even if in harness, lie dormant and can
be activated in the blink of an eye. Human praise,
at any level, should prove embarrassing for any person who has even a tinge of self-knowledge.

ACTION

Identify by name those passions that underlie your
thoughts, speech, and actions.

DAY THREE
Purity and Liberation

To be pure in heart means, among other things, to have freed yourself from all such half-measures: from a tone of voice which places you in the limelight, a furtive acceptance of some desire of the flesh which ignores the desire of the spirit, a self-righteous reaction to others in their moments of weakness.

The purer the eye of her attention, the more power the soul finds within herself. But it is very rare to find a soul who is entirely free, whose purity is not soiled by the stain of some secret desire of her own. Strive, then, constantly to purify the eye of your attention until it becomes utterly simple and direct.

—Dag Hammarskjold

REFLECTION

Purity and freedom are are twins, inseparable if not identical. Narcissism destroys purity: excessive self-preoccupation stains the eye and the soul in its being for others. Purity lived is liberation. No longer is the soul enslaved by passion or self-seeking, by self-referencing everything. When freedom comes with its twin, purity, we live simply and directly.

ACTION

By fasting one day a week both the soul and the body will be put on the path to freedom and liberation—yes, the path of purity.

DAY FOUR

Using God as a Candle

Know, too, that when you seek on your own, you never find God, for you are not seeking him with purity of heart. You are seeking something along with God and you act as if you were using God, as if he were a candle with which one might look for something else and, having found it, you might throw the candle away.

—Meister Eckhart

REFLECTION

Purity has to do with both desire and motivation. What is it that we are truly seeking and why? Tremendous honesty is demanded here. Much grace is needed to "purify" our motives and to be truthful about our longings. Otherwise, we use God as a means to an end and fall into the pit of idolatry.

ACTION

Light a candle and spend fifteen minutes gazing into its flame. Ask God to enlighten you to understand what it is that you are seeking and why.

Concupiscence of the Mind

...it is certain that mind is the principal thing. A mind consciously unclean cannot be cleansed by fasting. Modifications in diet have no effect on it. The concupiscence of the mind cannot be rooted out except by intense self-examination, surrender to God and, lastly, grace. But there is an intimate connection between the mind and the body, and the carnal mind always lusts for delicacies and luxuries. To obviate this tendency dietetic restrictions and fasting would appear to be necessary. The carnal mind, instead of controlling the senses, becomes their slave, and therefore the body always needs clean non-stimulating foods and periodical fasting.

—Mohandas K. Gandhi

REFLECTION

Concupiscence is a matter of both mind and body, and what touches one will necessarily have an effect on the other. The body/soul relationship is enigmatic and complex. We need to avoid a false dualism, yet it is clear that body and soul are not the same, that they differ, and that each has its own dynamic currents and principles. While the practice of fasting, in and of itself, will not eliminate the mind's uncontrolled passions, it will affect our cognition and knowing patterns in subtle and powerful ways. Fasting and the discipline of selective eating can help prevent the mind from being enslaved to the appetites.

ACTION

Monitor attentively the passions of the mind and body. Try to determine the effects—both positive and negative—that specific foods have on the well-being of body and mind.

Experiencing Things Reverently

Chastity is, first of all, not even primarily a sexual con-
cept, though, given the power and urgency of sex, faults
in chastity are often within the area of sexuality.
Chastity has to do with all experiencing. It is about the
appropriateness of any experience. Ultimately, chastity is
reverence—and sin, all sin, is irreverence. To be chaste is
to experience people, things, places, entertainment, the
phases of our lives, and sex in a way that does not
violate them or ourselves. To be chaste is to experience
things reverently, in such a way that the experience
leaves both them and ourselves more, not less, integrated.

—Ronald Rolheiser

REFLECTION

Reverence is at the core of chastity. Holding
sacred every breath, every word, every action is a
way of life that is essentially pure. Thus, hurry is
unchaste, as are putdowns and manipulation of
any order. Honoring everyone and everything—
standing on holy ground—is the Christian way of
life, one that is pure and chaste.

ACTION

Ask God to anoint every word and action with the
oil of grace. Try to experience everything, every
word and deed, in the light of God's presence.

Purity and Honest Beginnings

Purity of spirit lies at the beginning of things, there where the first stirrings set in, where conceptions of being and doing are formed. It is that initial authenticity in which the true meaning of words is grounded and their relation to each other is corrected, their edges are trimmed. Spirit becomes impure through essential dishonesty. When it attempts to call evil good, it becomes essentially corrupt.

—Romano Guardini

REFLECTION

Be it life itself or any particular instances of our existence, the beginning, the middle, and the end all have their value and their influence. Each has a different set of criteria for evaluation. But who would deny the incredible significance of how things begin: a marriage, a day, the start of a discourse, a particular season of the year. It is here that purity or corruption is planted; it is from that starting point that the fruit can be predicted. Every racer knows that the winner of most races is determined the second after "Get ready, get set, go!"

ACTION

Pause for fifteen to thirty seconds before writing a letter, making a phone call, opening a door for an encounter, and ask that what is said or done might take on the quality of pure, transparent honesty.

WEEK TWO

A Humble Heart
That I May Hear Thee!

CHRIST THE KING

His transport a donkey,
a beast of burden,
poor and humble.

His crown, a wreath of thorns,
and then for a throne,
a tree we call the cross.

His kingly return? Disguised as
a pilgrim, a gardener, a cook.
Royal, indeed!

Here is Christ the King,
poor, humble, glorious.

Why, according to C. S. Lewis, is listening such a difficult art for the human race? Perhaps it's because hearing demands humility. To hear requires a heart that knows the limits of knowledge and the inadequacy of words. Perhaps we find it difficult to hear the voice of the Risen Lord because we expect him to speak in ways other than that of a traveler who asks questions, or of a cook who serves.

Humility is a twin of poverty. It recognizes that all is given and that we can claim nothing as our own. Humility plunges us into the truth of things and, when lived deeply, turns us into grateful creatures. We rejoice in our dependency; we exult that our God sustains us every step of the way. Like the travelers on the way to Emmaus, we find our hearts burning within us as our humble, regal King accompanies us on our journey through life.

DAY ONE
Humility = Sense of Reality

Humility, indeed, is simply a sense of reality and proportion.
It is grounded upon a knowledge of the truth about ourselves
and about God.

—*Brigid E. Herman*

REFLECTION

In her poem "Mirror," Sylvia Plath says that mirrors don't lie. They are "silver and exact." To see accurately, without distortion, all of reality—be it others, yourself, or God—is extremely difficult. Our glasses are tinted; our assumptions and presumptions numerous; our prejudices blinding. We need much grace if we are to have a sense of proportion and reality. Though truth is elusive, we can know and rejoice in the truth that will set us free.

ACTION

Spend five minutes looking quietly into a mirror. Ask for the grace of self-knowledge and the charism of humility.

DAY TWO
"Unless you become..."

In the child's attitude lies his humility: as Jesus says, he does not count himself for much. He does not drag his small ego into the foreground; his consciousness brims with objects, people, events—not himself.

—Romano Guardini

REFLECTION

Self-referential living is a constant dragging of oneself to center stage. How annoying to others and, indeed, to oneself. Children lost in play, caught up in the glory of the moment, are gifted with blessed self-unconsciousness. Though this will change as the years pass, for the moment their lives brim with something other than their small ego. Humility does not undervalue who we are, for while in our own eyes we might not count for much, in God's eyes we do.

ACTION

Pause to watch children at play, be it at recess at school or at the city park. Use your imagination to enter into their world and then pray for grace of a non-self-referential life.

DAY THREE
Humility: Two Causes

In itself, humility is nothing else but a man's true understanding and awareness of himself as he really is. It is certain that if a man could truly see and be conscious of himself as he really is, he would indeed be truly humble. There are two causes of this meekness: one is the foulness, wretchedness and weakness into which a man has fallen by sin. As long as he lives in this life, no matter how holy he is, he must always experience this in some measure. The other is the superabundant love and worthiness of God himself. At the sight of this, all nature trembles, all learned men are fools, and all the saints and angels are blinded; so much so that were it not for the wisdom of his Godhead, whereby due proportion is set between their contemplation and their natural and grace-given capacity, I would be at a loss to say what would happen to them.

—The Cloud of Unknowing

REFLECTION

It seems incredible that some of the great saints and mystics of the church, like St. Paul and St. Teresa of Avila, identify themselves as the greatest of sinners. Yet, they have good cause. In fact, two great causes. One is a deep awareness of their own sin. The other is their experience of God's extravagant and unconditional love. Anyone who is truly in touch with these two *facts* can only be be humble and meek. The problem is fixation. St. Paul and St. Teresa of Avila avoided getting caught in their own sinful nature; they were graced to focus on the mercy and love of God as revealed in Jesus. They were graced with the virtue of humility.

ACTION

Read Isaiah 43 and ponder the mystery of God's love. Read Galatians 5 and name your own areas of sin.

Humility: Taking God's Hand

Humility means that a man resolves to take God's hand with trust in his guidance: that he becomes little with the little ones, honours the old, shows courtesy to women, keeps unpleasantness from others, takes the weak under the protection of his strength, moderates the movements of inner violence, lightens life for others, so that no evil befalls them.

—*Ladislaus Boros*

REFLECTION

Humility has an active side. Once we are grasped by the Lord, taken by the hand, we share in the qualities of our Triune God. Like Jesus, we become little by participating in his poverty. Like Julian of Norwich's God, we are to be supremely courteous toward all. Like Cardinal Newman's gentleman, we are sensitive to what is unpleasant for others and compassionate toward the weak. Like the great Hindu, Gandhi, we strive for that inner gentleness that deals with our violence. Like Mother Teresa of Calcutta, we do whatever we can to lighten the burdens of others. Beneath all these attitudes and behaviors resides the grace of a humble heart.

ACTION

Identify a neighbor, a co-worker, or an acquaintance who is suffering and seek today to lighten that person's burden.

DAY FIVE
A Great Disparity

If you are looking about for things to even out the
disparity between the brains of ordinary animals and
the great minds of ourselves, the superprimate humans,
this apparatus is a good one to reflect on in humility.
Compared to the common dog, or any rodent in the field,
we are primitive, insensitive creatures, biological failures.
Heaven knows how much of the world we are missing.

—Lewis Thomas

REFLECTION

Failures tend to promote humility, sometimes humiliation. Thus, when a scientist informs us that we are biological failures compared to the common dog, the rat in the corner, the eagle in the sky, the deer in the meadow—well, we might want to cover our faces in shame. Our five senses lack the capacity to "pick up" so much of life that our fellow creatures apprehend with ease. The speed of the gazelle, the strength of the gorilla, the sight of the hawk should instill in the fastest runner, the strongest wrestler, and the ablest marksman a sense of honest humility.

ACTION

Watch for a hawk today or observe a dog in the neighborhood. How do you compare with them in attentiveness to reality?

The Art of Saying "Yes"

Many years ago I heard a functional definition of humility
which sheds more and more light the longer I live.
Humility, it said, is the willingness to be what you are
and to do what you can. Accordingly, the humble man
does not merely recognize what he is. In itself such
recognition is an act of the intellect. But the humble
man does more than that. In the depth of his being, he
consents to, affirms, ratifies and says yes to what he is.

—*Joseph Gallagher*

REFLECTION

The gap between knowledge and acknowledgement is often wide. Mere intellectual comprehension—that we are finite, limited, sinful creatures—is light years away from the embrace of that reality in the depths of our being. True humility bridges the gap so that our hearts can grasp what our minds know. The journey we must make is a painful one, requiring harsh transformation. Yet that is the agency of humility: to get us to say "yes" to who we are and to what we can and cannot do.

ACTION

Ask a friend to name one of your gifts and one of your limitations. Have you said "yes" to both in your heart?

The Proud Person, the Humble Person

A proud man envies the superiority which surpasses him. A humble one, on the contrary, loves good wherever he finds it, and by this love, in some sense appropriates it to himself.

—Raissa Maritain

REFLECTION

In the presence of what is superior—a brilliant mind, a more beautiful body, a more gifted athlete —how does one's heart respond? Envy and jealousy arise from pride; delight and enjoyment from humility. In a culture of individualism, lacking a sense of common humanity, we see others as competitors. What others have, we lack. In a culture of the common good, of solidarity, we know that others' gifts benefit us all. Individualism engenders pride; solidarity fosters the grace of humility.

ACTION

Compliment a fellow worker or member of your family for a gift that person possesses.

WEEK THREE

A Heart of Love
That I May Serve Thee!

A PATCH OF HOLINESS

Our torn, tattered history needs patching,
pieces of love to cover the tears,
fabric of affection to heal our hardness of heart.
And patches have come.
Francis mended his times with troubadour songs,
Mother Teresa with hospice care.
Patches of love holding together
whole nations on the edge of disintegration.
Whether Italy or India,
Wall Street or the monastery,
the halls of parliament or the university dorm,
we need a patch of holiness,
a light to shine in our dark universe.

Love does more than make the world go round. It also
heals and mends what has been broken and torn. Love is
the power that transforms and renews, refreshes, and
cleanses. Love is of God; indeed, God is Love. Nothing is
more vital than to be given a heart of love, a heart that
then allows the Lord to serve others through us. All the

saints knew deep down that it was not their loving that wrought salvation but the loving Lord working in and through them. Love is more than a many-splendored thing. In the end, it is everything. To be loved and to love is at the core of human and divine happiness. To be loved is grace; to love is to be gracious because one is graced.

DAY ONE

Love's Many Meanings and Shapes

We all know that the word love has many meanings. For some, love is primarily romantic; for others, love is primarily physical; still others interpret love as selflessness; some strive for purely spiritual love which leaves behind the world's hustle and bustle. Love, however, has not only many meanings but several shapes.

There is the love between husband and wife, the love of parents for their children, and children for their parents. There is love in religious communities and in parish communities. There is love among friends.

Jean Vanier...points to the core when he describes love as "revealing to someone else that person's own beauty." Love means showing the other how beautiful he or she is. The other person cannot discover this alone; even a mirror will not suffice. Another human being is needed. When that happens, love is realized.

—Peter van Breeman, SJ

REFLECTION

We might add other meanings of love to the above: the tough love that is willing to confront destructive patterns in others; love for one's country; love for the graciousness of creation; love for sports and gardening and books; the list goes on and on and on. So too the shapes and expressions of love: the pat on the back; the midsummer picnics with family; the phone call to comfort someone in pain or mourning a loss; the hug and the kiss; the holding of hands. Love is, indeed, a many-splendored thing and no thought or number of words can begin to exhaust its meanings or manifestations.

ACTION

Call someone today or send a note telling that person how beautiful he or she is.

The Greatest Secret: Love

A thought transfixed me: for the first time in my life I
saw the truth as it is set into song by so many poets,
proclaimed as the final wisdom by so many thinkers.
The truth—that love is the ultimate and the highest
goal to which man can aspire. Then I grasped the mean-
ing of the greatest secret that human poetry and human
thought and belief have to impart: the salvation of man
is through love and in love. I understood how a man who
has nothing left in this world still may know bliss, be it
only for a brief moment, in the contemplation of his
beloved. In a position of utter desolation, when man
cannot express himself in positive action, when his only
achievement may consist in enduring his sufferings in
the right way—an honorable way—in such a position
man can, through loving contemplation of the image he
carries of his beloved, achieve fulfillment. For the first
time in my life I was able to understand the meaning of
the words, "The angels are lost in perpetual contemplation
of an infinite glory."

—Viktor E. Frankl

REFLECTION

Poets and philosophers, prophets and pilgrims,
have all been in search of the ultimate secret and
the meaning of life. Our hunger to know is
matched only by our hunger to love and be loved.
Viktor Frankl, enduring the horrors of a concentration camp, came to an insight into life's ultimate

truth—the mystery and grace of love. Indeed, salvation comes to us through the love of God; indeed, the world is redeemed to the extent that we receive that love and share it with others. If contemplation is nothing other than "loving attention," then we have here the way of life that puts us in a position to experience life's meaning, wisdom, and grace.

ACTION

Spend fifteen minutes today in silence, reflecting lovingly upon the people who have loved you and the people you have loved.

Love Alone

*Love alone makes man forget himself, and it would
indeed be hell if such self-oblivion could never be
achieved. Love alone can redeem even the darkest
hours of the past, since love alone is brave enough
to believe in the mercy of God. Love alone does not
selfishly hold back: it is therefore able to dispose even
of the future. Without love, man, anxiously guarding
his finite Ego, would husband his future and yield it
but grudgingly. Love alone can, as it were, draw God
on to this earth, thus integrating all earthly love in
the moment of eternity. To love alone, therefore, is
given that persistency of courage which loves Him
Who sees, through guilt, failure and death, the bravery
of His creature.*

—Karl Rahner

REFLECTION

Love is highly pragmatic; it is not static but
active. It multiplies things and gives birth to
other things. For example, it produces blessed
self-forgetfulness, or gives us the courage to say
"yes" to the future or believe in God's infinite
mercy and love. Love works! It is an energy that
transforms minds and history, indeed, human history. Devoid of the grace of love, we stumble and
stutter our way through life, knowing no peace or
joy. Love has the quality of eternity and immortality. As Emily Dickinson correctly observes,

"Unable are the Loved to die...
Unable they that love—to die."

ACTION

Write down on a piece of paper a few words describing "the darkest hour" of your life. After you have done this, write on the reverse: "I believe in God's mercy."

DAY FOUR
The Loving Heart of Christ

*Let us love those near by and those afar; love our own
country and those others; love our friends and enemies;
love Catholics, schismatics, Protestants, Anglicans, the
indifferent; love Moslems, pagans, atheists; love members
of all social classes, particularly those most in need of
help and support; love children; love the old, the poor
and the sick; love those who deride or despise us, obstruct
or persecute us; love those who deserve love and those
who do not; love our adversaries—we want no man as our
enemy; love our own times, our modern civilization,
techniques, art, sport, our world. Let us love and try to
understand, esteem, appreciate, serve it and suffer for it.
Let us love it with the heart of Christ.*

—Pope Paul VI (Cardinal Montini)

REFLECTION

Most of our loving is selective and exclusive. We
choose the people we want to love, excluding the
undesirables from our affection and avoiding
those who are unpleasant and antagonistic toward
us. How far we are from that inclusive, universal
love manifested in the life of Jesus! Much grace is
needed if we are to begin to embrace with respect
and concern every person we encounter on this
strange journey called life. St. Paul encourages us
to put on the mind and heart of Christ. Only by
doing this will we have the clarity of mind to see all
people the way Christ sees them and the largeness

of heart to live out our discipleship of loving and forgiving.

ACTION

Reach out—by, for example, sending a note—to an "enemy," someone who has offended you. Through this gesture of openness and love, healing may come.

Life Is Not Life without Love

*Service meant at best the material amelioration of the
lot of man; the metaphysical tradition has been lost.
Christianity, like the nineteenth century, believed in
progress; believed in the search for happiness and perfection; believed therefore that it was the destiny of man to
achieve the perfection of his personality on every level of
life. But it believed that the process of perfection must
be subsumed under a deeper, and at first sight paradoxical, quest: the quest for self-loss in God. The creature is
perfect only when his proper perfection is subordinated
to his creaturely relationship with the Creator. It is not
a question of ethical unselfishness; it is far deeper than
that. It is simply the deepest and most irrefutable of all
human facts: that life is not life unless it is love, and
that love consists essentially not in getting but in giving,
and primarily, giving not material things but the spirit,
the self. Only by self-loss in the Infinite is the thirst for
the Infinite quenched; and when that is denied to man
he will look for other objects in the finite world and,
since they are finite, they will not suffice. Hence restless-
ness, confusion, pessimism; and it is to these things and
not to the peace that surpasseth understanding that
nineteenth-century optimism has led us. For nothing
could be more alien to an anthropocentric world, con-
vinced that nothing existed except what science could
apprehend and explain, than the notion of such a metaphysical emptying of selfhood.*

—Gerald Vann

REFLECTION

Making the world a better place is certainly a Christian imperative. We have the abiding duty to assist all those in need at every level of existence. But that ethical work is but the first step in the journey toward the meaning of life. Deeper than doing is the mystery of being. Love leads to a self-emptying for the well-being of others; love connects us to the Source of our existence. It is in this total self-giving that true perfection lies, that is, the place of holiness. Anything short of the giving of self to the will of God will lead to confusion and anxiety. The grace of love alone brings the peace beyond scientific and psychological understanding.

ACTION

Find a copy of George Herbert's poem "Love— III" and commit it to memory.

Loving and Praying

Farewell, farewell! but this I tell
To Thee, thou Wedding-Guest!
He prayeth well, who loveth well
Both man and bird and beast.

He prayeth best, who loveth best
All things both great and small;
For the dear God who loveth us,
He made and loveth all.

—Samuel Taylor Coleridge

REFLECTION

Poets are at times theologians. Coleridge offers an insight regarding the authenticity of our prayer. A person and community pray best when love is expressed in active concern for others. By contrast, to pray daily and to worship with the community weekly yet to fail to be deeply concerned about the well-being of others raises serious questions about the quality and sincerity of that prayer. The poet challenges us to make love universal, loving our fellow human beings as well as the birds of the air and the beasts in the field. A heart of love does not compartmentalize charity in any way.

ACTION

Reflect on how your prayer life finds expression in loving deeds. Does your love embrace all of creation?

The Tenderness and Truth of Love

In this interior union God communicates Himself to the soul with such genuine love that no mother's affection, in which she tenderly caresses her child, nor brother's love, nor friendship is comparable to it. The tenderness and truth of love by which the immense Father favors and exalts this humble and loving soul reaches such a degree—O wonderful thing, worthy of all our awe and admiration!—that the Father Himself becomes subject to her for her exaltation, as though He were her servant and she His lord. And He is as solicitous in favoring her as He would be if He were her slave and she His god. So profound is the humility and sweetness of God!

—St. John of the Cross

REFLECTION

Were St. John of the Cross not a doctor of the church, we might think of the above passage as bordering on heresy. God the slave and servant of a humble, loving soul? Yet, what profound truth there is in this insight! Love does strange things, such as making Divinity "vulnerable" to a soul that is totally self-giving. No human love can compare to God's immense, extravagant love for the soul that is obedient and affectionate.

ACTION

Read Isaiah 43 twice. Spend fifteen minutes letting this image of God soak into your heart.

WEEK FOUR

A Heart of Faith
That I May Abide in Thee!

FAITH

Some say faith comes and goes,
has a certain instability in the human heart,
sometimes "slips and laughs and rallies."
But not so "caring,"
a love and concern for others,
meeting the needs of the poor and suffering.

Here is a constant,
once possessed,
that centers and anchors our lives.
No mood or season,
no weather front or fad,
can tarnish a caring heart.

Yes, pray for faith.
Even more, care and share
and God will be found.

The chicken and the egg dilemma has never been resolved. And what about the faith and love dilemma: Which comes first? Is love the parent of faith or is it the other way around? And then throw hope into the mix and we need a mighty theologian to untangle the enigma.

St. Paul reminds us that in the end faith and hope will go; it is love that remains. So, if you have to put all your eggs in one basket, opt for the basket of charity. Yet it is faith that opens the heart to the mystery of God's love and mercy. Yet it is hope that enables us to trust and have confidence in God's promise of loving presence. We don't need a theologian to unravel this truth.

An ounce of faith will do it. It is sufficient to expose us to the radiance of God's extravagant benevolence. Our challenge is to abide in the light and turn away from darkness. To do this is to experience salvation.

Evangelical Faith

Faith, as we understand it here, is not—of course—simply the intellectual adherence to Christian dogma. It is taken in a much richer sense to mean belief in God charged with all the trust in his beneficent strength that the knowledge of the divine Being arouses in us. It means the practical conviction that the universe, between the hands of the Creator, still continues to be the clay in which he shapes innumerable possibilities according to his will. In a word, it is evangelical faith, of which it can be said that no virtue, not even charity, was more strongly urged by the Saviour.

—Teilhard de Chardin

REFLECTION

Two words that circle the heart of faith are trust and conviction. God is trustworthy; God deserves our commitment. We are here at the experiential level, miles beyond just intellectual acceptance of a system of beliefs. God is trustworthy because we can look back over our lives and perceive countless graces. God deserves our commitment because he continues to invite us to participate in building the kingdom. In the end, charity remains. But, until then, it is faith that unites us to God who is Love.

ACTION

Make a commitment today to a generous "yes" to every event—be it joyful or painful, delightful or distressing—that comes your way.

DAY TWO
Attitude or Achievement

The emphasis must be not upon achievement but upon attitude. What holds a life together is simply the truth— or faith—that the eyes and the heart are turned towards truth, and that God accepts such a life without condition, looking on the will rather than merely the deed. God asks not for heroes but for lovers; not moral athletes but men and women aware of their need for acceptance, ready to find their selfhood in the longing for communion with an eternal "other."

—*Rowan Williams*

REFLECTION

One of the deepest hungers of the human heart is for wholeness, a graced integrity. Often we may think that this is evidenced by achievement and a perfect moral life. Yet what holds a life together (integrity) is a deep, abiding faith and trust in God who is truth. We long for intimacy with God and it is faith and trust that bring us to that door. Relying on heroic, moral achievement means setting ourselves up for failure.

ACTION

Talk with someone today about the difference between achievement and attitudes. Further, talk about what holds your life together.

God: True Artisan of Faith

*Behind the impenetrable obscurity which envelops the
beginning of faith there lies an even profounder mystery:
faith is the work of God. All those efforts of thought, those
instances of perception, those emotions caused by religious
values, those encounters with the saints, are the materials
in which the true artisan, God, accomplishes his work.
Becoming a believer is the effect of a divine action which
touches, transforms, illumines, draws us, while remaining
shrouded in the mystery of grace. No psychological analysis,
no logical reasoning can penetrate there.*

—Romano Guardini

REFLECTION

Any farmer, as he brings in the acres of corn at harvest time, is keenly aware that, although he planted
and cultivated the fields, it was nature that pro-
duced the bountiful yield. Any believer, dwelling for
a moment upon the gift and mystery of faith, real-
izes that this grace is ultimately the accomplishment
of a creative God. Nor does this realization put
down the importance of study, reflection, or even a
strong emotional life. It is simply dealing with the
truth of God's artisanship in our spiritual life.

ACTION

Draw a picture of your faith. What does it look
like and who is the true designer?

DAY FOUR
Endangered Faith

Faith can be lost. Because faith is a free response, not coerced either by rational evidence or by the gifts of grace, it can be renounced. In the circumstances of today's world, faith is especially imperiled by the climate of secularism, the erosion of traditional sociological supports, the rapidity of cultural change, the aggressive propagation of alternative belief-systems, and the bewildering variety of contemporary options.

—Avery Dulles, SJ

REFLECTION

Life—be it the physical life of an infant, the psychological life of a vulnerable teenager, the intellectual life of a university student, or the spiritual life of a believing disciple—is fragile and demands protection. There are forces, such as physical violence, disrespect, skepticism, or rampant atheism, that can injure and even destroy these forms of life. Our faith life can be threatened by various movements and trends in any given culture. We must be aware of each of them and seek to nurture our faith by discipline and participation in communities that are life-giving.

ACTION

Strengthen the faith of a friend this day by sharing one of your favorite scriptural passages and asking your friend to do the same with you.

DAY FIVE
Communicating Faith

You told me that [although] you had been a believing and practicing Christian,... you had ceased to believe and to worship. But you hoped that I would help you to recover your faith. Thank God I did not attempt to instruct you or argue with you, for even in the days of my young manhood I believed that this was the most barren way of communicating faith. So I attempted to communicate faith to you by loving you, wholeheartedly and tenderly, and as unselfishly as I knew how. It was given to me to be generous in love, but now I surpassed myself, and to you to whom desolation had come so suddenly it was like a reparation, and you warmed to me in gratitude.

—Alan Paton

REFLECTION

G. K. Chesterton defended the faith with eloquent words. John Henry Cardinal Newman wrote about faith with great rationality. Faith can be communicated through theological language and intricate argumentation. But, for most people, faith comes through the door of tender love and gracious hospitality, quietly slipping into the human heart and doing its work of transformation.

ACTION

Contact a family or community member to express your love and concern. Invite that person to attend a worship service with you.

DAY SIX

The Fittingness of Things

The winter hills nourish my faith. There had been no
emotional upheaval, no great insight, certainly no grasp
of theological issues; just a sense of history and the
fittingness of things. Something impossible to explain.
Pere Teilhard Chardin says, "The incommunicable part
of us is the pasture of God." I must leave it at that.

—*Alec Guinness*

REFLECTION

> Faith is nourished in many ways: the pondering of
> scripture, the celebration of the sacraments, walk-
> ing the winter hills. Our relationship with God is
> fed in thousands of ways, ways that are often
> incommunicable but nonetheless real. To explain
> the origin and growth of faith is as difficult as
> attempting to capture beauty in a poem. Mystery
> upon mystery. In the end it is the experience of
> peace—the fittingness of things.

ACTION

> Walk the hills around you and let your faith be
> nourished.

DAY SEVEN
The Knight of Faith

Kierkegaard had his own formula for what it means to be a man. He put it forth in those superb pages wherein he describes what he calls "the knight of faith." This figure is the man who lives in faith, who has given over the meaning of life to his Creator, and who lives centered on the energies of his Maker. He accepts whatever happens in his visible dimension without complaint, lives his life as a duty, faces death without a qualm. No pettiness is so petty that it threatens his meanings; no task is too frightening to be beyond his courage. He is fully in the world on its terms and wholly beyond the world in his trust in the invisible dimension. It is very much the old Pietistic ideal that was lived by Kant's parents. The great strength of such an ideal is that it allows one to be open, generous, courageous, to touch others' lives and enrich them and open them in turn. As the knight of faith has no fear-of-life-and-death to lay onto others, he does not cause them to shrink back upon themselves, he does not coerce or manipulate them. The knight of faith, then, represents what we might call an ideal of mental health, the continuing openness of life out of the death throes of dread.

—Ernest Becker

REFLECTION

Death is ubiquitous. So too is the fear and denial of it—except for the person of deep faith. Left to our own human ingenuity, we realize quickly that we are powerless in the face of the mystery of death. In fact, for many individuals, death ends everything and tends to make the human journey meaningless, since there is no destination other than annihilation. By contrast, faith interprets death as liberation. Death takes us out of the "shadowlands" and into the fullness of life. Would that we all had a king who would knight us with the gift of faith. But then, in fact, we do in the kingship of Jesus.

ACTION

Call an acquaintance who has lost a loved one during the past year. If appropriate, share some aspect of your faith with the person you have called.

A Heart of Courage
That I May Follow Thee!

LEWIS & CLARK

They journeyed west,
into the deep unknown.
They lost but one man
in the two-and-a-half year expedition.
Rivers and mountains,
prairies and plains,
traversed at great cost and sacrifice.
And in the end?
New knowledge of plants and animals,
new maps of lands and rivers,
and, most of all,
a witness to undaunted courage.

Just as explorers venture into new terrain, so too the great spiritual guides have opened new frontiers for the rest of us, the more shy pilgrims. Think of such saints as Augustine of Hippo and Ignatius of Loyola, John of the Cross and Teresa of Avila. The list of disciples of the Lord who exemplified undaunted courage goes on and on. Having set their hands to the plow, they followed where Christ led.

In the end it always comes back to suffering and death and how those experiences are embraced. In the end, it is a participation in the mystery of the cross. And just as the invitation is offered to journey with Christ into self-giving love, so the grace is also offered, because without divine assistance we will stumble and fall. We ask for a heart of courage, the kind that St. Paul had, so that by sharing in the sufferings of Christ we might experience the joy of new life.

DAY ONE

The Indispensable Virtue

I ran away from my first fight. In those days I did not know that courage is the indispensable virtue. Life had not yet taught me that, without courage, kindness and compassion remain merely fatuous postures.

—Whittaker Chambers

As [Samuel] Johnson points out, where courage is not, no other virtue can survive, except by accident.

—C. S. Lewis

REFLECTION

Fear is a predominant emotion on this planet. Many forces—natural disasters, psychological rejection, spiritual abandonment—confront us and our initial tendency is flight. We run from danger; indeed, we run from life, because it is so threatening, and thereby never live. Courage is the ability to hang in there, to face danger, to engage our suffering, to risk rejection, and so much more. To dispense with courage is to dispense with moral character. Courage is the *sine qua non* of being truly human.

ACTION

Call to mind a situation that you have been avoiding for years. Ask for the grace of courage and address the issue before the sun sets.

Seeing Things Through

"I wanted you to see something about her—I wanted you to see what real courage is, instead of getting the idea that courage is a man with a gun in his hand. It's when you know you're licked before you begin but you begin anyway and you see it through no matter what. You rarely win, but sometimes you do. Mrs. Dubose won, all ninety-eight pounds of her. According to her views, she died beholden to nothing and nobody. She was the bravest person I ever knew."

—*Atticus Finch in Harper Lee's* To Kill a Mockingbird

REFLECTION

John the Baptist never had a chance as he came up against the power of Herod and his regime. He was licked before he began, but that did not stop him from fulfilling his prophetic role. He would preach repentance no matter what; he would invite people into the truth regardless of the threat to his own person. Archbishop Oscar Romero was another courageous prophet; he spoke out for the voiceless in San Salvador. His assassination gives proof of his courage.

ACTION

Write a note to someone whom you see as having been a witness to courage. Thank that person for being a model of discipleship.

Courage for Life

This, then, is what courage means, courage for life, for real living. The essence of the virtue of courage doesn't lie in attack, self-reliance, or anger, but in patient endurance. That is so not because patience and endurance are better and more perfect in themselves than active self-reliance, but because the real world is made up of contradictions to the point where man can only call on his greatest and deepest powers of soul on occasions of such seriousness that no possibility of struggle remains, and there is nothing left save endurance. Patience is very different from the passive acceptance of all evils that come. Aquinas wrote: "The patient man is not one who doesn't see evil, but one who doesn't let it force him into sadness." To be patient means not to let one's soul be robbed of its gaiety and clarity of vision by the sufferings that are part of the working out of salvation.

—Ladislaus Boros

REFLECTION

No one is exempt from experiencing evil and the mystery of suffering. It is part, often a major part, of the human condition. The question arises: How do we respond? The courageous person, gifted by God's grace, engages the dark side of his or her life with patience and endurance. The courageous person refuses to become angry and embittered; the courageous person embraces hardship with nobility. And when God's grace is really strong in the soul, joy and "clarity of vision" remain.

ACTION

Spend five minutes in prayerful contemplation of the crucified Christ. Ask yourself: How was it possible for the Lord to endure patiently such a horrendous experience?

DAY FOUR
Shouldering the Burden of Self

Above all, we have got to have courage with ourselves,
with our dark, unattractive natures that oppose all
we long to be and do. That means to shoulder the
burden of our own psyche's disability—wrong impulses,
reluctance, and fears—and to face the instinctive
tendencies that seem too strong for us and war against
our best minds. So we go on as we must, letting the
wheat and the tares grow together to the end, saying
within the conflict, "Thou understandest my thoughts
afar off!" We don't understand. But we go through life
with confidence because God understands that obsessive,
impulsive difficulty which we don't understand. For
we know that even through [such things], He can guide
and discipline us.

—Evelyn Underhill

REFLECTION

Getting in touch with our shadow side is not easy.
Embracing that dark dimension, even though we
lack total understanding, is even more daunting.
Yet these are exactly the things that courage enables us to do. Courage gives us the power to
identify and take responsibility for those tendencies and characteristics of ours that are neither
pleasant for us nor enriching for others. This is
not a case of complacency. Rather, it is the nobility of naming what is and working with our limitations. Within all this self-reflection we turn to our

merciful and loving God in whom we find our strength and our hope.

ACTION

Take the time to share with a trusted friend some personal burden that is weighing you down. Let God's healing grace come to you through that conversation.

A Decline in Courage

A decline in courage may be the most striking feature which an outside observer notices in the West in our days. The Western world has lost its civil courage, both as a whole and separately, in each country, each government, and each political party and of course in the United Nations. Such a decline in courage is particularly noticeable among the ruling groups and the intellectual elite, causing an impression of loss of courage by the entire society. Of course there are many courageous individuals but they have no determining influence on public life. Political and intellectual bureaucrats show depression, passivity and perplexity in their actions and in their statements and even more so in theoretical reflections to explain how realistic, reasonable as well as intellectually and even morally warranted it is to base state policies on weakness and cowardice. And decline in courage is ironically emphasized by occasional explosions of anger and inflexibility on the part of the same bureaucrats when dealing with weak governments and weak countries, not supported by anyone, or with currents which cannot offer any resistance. But they get tongue-tied and paralyzed when they deal with powerful governments and threatening forces, with aggressors and international terrorists.

Should one point out that from ancient times decline in courage has been considered the beginning of the end?

—Alexander Solzhenitsyn

REFLECTION

Weakness and cowardice have forever been a part of the human condition. But so have courage and fortitude. In doing a social analysis, some analysts conclude that courage is on the decline, if not totally lost. Plenty of evidence can be accumulated to support this judgment. But there are also many noble and outstanding citizens and communities of people who are willing to sacrifice their very lives in the defense of freedom and truth. Sweeping statements do not serve us well. History, like the human heart, is ambiguous. Everyone is engaged in a fierce conflict between courage and cowardice.

ACTION

Read an article on Abraham Lincoln or Oscar Romero or Dorothy Day. How did they respond with courage to their situations?

DAY SIX
The Gift of Courage

Cowardly Lion:
> *Courage! What makes a king out of a slave? Courage!*
> *What makes the flag on the mast to wave? Courage!*
> *What makes the elephant charge his tusk in the misty*
> *mist, or the dusky dusk? What makes the muskrat*
> *guard his musk? Courage! What makes the sphinx the*
> *seventh wonder? Courage! What makes the dawn come*
> *up like thunder? Courage! What makes the Hottentot so*
> *hot? What puts the "ape" in apricot? What have they got*
> *that I ain't got?*

Dorothy, Scarecrow, Tin Woodsman:
> *Courage!*

Cowardly Lion:
> *You can say that again! Hunh!*

> —*Song from* The Wizard of Oz

REFLECTION

Dorothy travels through the land of Oz with companions who lack some essential things: a brain, a heart, courage. They depend on her for knowledge, love, and the ability to act. The great king of the forest, the lion, has turned out to be cowardly. Although he knows some of the characteristics of courage, he himself lacks them all. Dorothy will supply what is lacking and bring her companions to journey's end.

ACTION

Watch the film *The Wizard of Oz* and see how many examples of courage you can find in it.

Courage and Fear

Courage is not the absence of fear; it is the making of action in spite of fear, the moving out against the resistance engendered by fear into the unknown and into the future. On some level spiritual growth, and therefore love, always requires courage and involves risk.

—M. Scott Peck

REFLECTION

When Lewis and Clark set out in 1803 toward the Pacific Northwest, they ventured into the unknown, taking great risks. How fitting that Stephen Ambrose's excellent narration of this expedition was called *Undaunted Courage*. Surely, those two leaders and their crew of forty must have been frightened time and time again by the hostile forces of nature and their own inner demons. Yet they acted; they persisted and two and a half years later returned to St. Louis having demonstrated to the nation, and now history, what courage looks like in action.

ACTION

Look one of your fears in the face and decide to confront it by some fitting action before the sun sets today.

WEEK SIX

A Heart of Joy
That I May Sing with Thee!

JOY

It's like the wind
    blowing now here, now there,
    wherever people care,
    where the right thing is done
      in the right way.

It's like sunshine,
    falling on every flower, every atom
    so that petals open and expand
    and every atom dances, doing handstands.

It's like an infant's smile,
    tickled into laughter,
    hugged into life,
    wrapped in the warmth of a grandma's arms.

Joy is like, well, like
    a love letter carried next to the heart.

I've seen it time and time again, at airports, at bus depots,
at train stations. I've seen the joy of welcome when child
and parent, friend and friend, husband and wife are once

more reunited, enfolded in a loving embrace. Often there are tears, those tears of joy that flow directly from the heart. And there is music in the air, the melody of love's return.

To have a heart of joy that enables us to sing of God's love is a deep expression of discipleship. The great model is St. Paul, especially in his letter to the Philippians. Despite his many sufferings and burdens, Paul urges the community of Philippi to rejoice, to rejoice always in the Lord. That biblical joy is grounded in the person of Jesus and his offer of love and mercy. Paul could sing because he saw. He saw through his trials and perceived the abiding presence of Christ.

This kind of joy is not ephemeral. It has about it the quality of eternity, and necessarily so, because joy is the offspring of love.

DAY ONE
Agents of Joy

...Perhaps most significantly, joy is a defining characteristic of the life of God. The parables of Luke 15 remind us that God also rejoices when those who were lost are found. God has always longed for the reconciliation of all creation. Thus when some parts of that creation are restored to their proper relation to God, God takes great delight. The parables of the lost sheep, the lost coin and the lost son all emphasize in their own way this profound truth: God rejoices when those who are estranged are restored. If God's life is marked by such joy, how can the lives of those who are called to embody God's character be any less joyful?

—Philip D. Kenneson

REFLECTION

Lostness—to be cut off from our lifelines, to be abandoned in this vast universe, to make a wrong turn down a dead-end alley—the very thought causes a hollowness in the pit of the stomach. But when we are found or when we find another, what joy in that glorious reunion! Our God is a God of unity and the divine will is for oneness, a union that causes profound joy. One of our tasks as disciples is to be reconcilers and thus be agents of joy, thereby emulating the very nature of God.

ACTION

Write a note to an individual who helped find you when you were lost.

A Measure of Joy

I no longer believe we can slug out a lifetime of Christian witness by placing our total offering on an altar marked "obligation." There has got to be a measure of joy in what we do, an anticipation of excitement when we face the day, rather than a dull feeling of boredom or resentment at what lies ahead. Some may call this "selfish" (Calvinists immediately begin to cover their tracks), but I am surer and surer that unless there is joy in what we do, the results will not only be drab and cheerless for us but also for those with whom we work.

—Robert McAfee Brown

REFLECTION

In his autobiographical work *My Experiments with Truth,* Gandhi wrote convincingly that work does not benefit either the served or the servant unless joy is present to some degree. One can sense immediately, both within others as well as oneself, when something is being done begrudgingly. An atmosphere is created that is ponderous, uncomfortable, and so often unproductive. Whatever one is called to do (or to endure), some measure of joy is essential if life is to have any quality.

ACTION

Take time to assess the degree of joy you put into this day's tasks.

The Demon of Joylessness

The third obstacle to living meekly stems from the tendency to see only what is wrong in a situation and never to affirm the good. This trait breeds a joylessness that lacks beatitude. We become literally killjoys, murdering that spirit of lightheartedness that signifies union with God. Without joy, we can never experience carefree playing before the face of the Father. If we do not know how to play, we may be unable to pray. We exude displeasure and are prone to pick fights. Others perceive a hostile streak in us. We are prone to insult people. We lack patience. What flows from our mouths is not blessing but barbs of bitterness. Joyless as we are, we find it nearly impossible to bestow kind words on others. We lack human warmth and seem to be angry at ourselves and the world.

—Susan Muto

REFLECTION

The profile of joylessness is clear and distasteful: bitter, impatient, pugnacious, hostile, cold, and aloof—all "killjoy" qualities. By contrast, joy is buoyant and warm, lighthearted, gracious, and life-giving. By creating an atmosphere of play, it opens the door to the possibility of happiness. More, it serves as a symbol of dwelling in God's presence, of becoming a conduit of the very joy of God. The ability to affirm what is good while not neglecting what is wrong is another characteristic of the joyful person. Could it be that joy makes prayer possible?

ACTION

Get in touch with someone who has shared human warmth with you, who has brought joy to your life. Thank that individual for being a gift and a blessing.

DAY FOUR
Introductory and Perfected Joy

Thus, between an "introductory joy" and a "perfected joy"
there is a "sadness dear to God." The soul would never
enter into the struggle in which it is "tested" if an initial
joy did not summon it. With this, the whole difference
between the first and the perfected experience of joy is
already expressed; the first joy is an initial experience of
the Ground of Being, but still not by far its full realiza-
tion, comparable to the winter sun, which warms those
exposed to it only on one side. This is why that first joy
can easily be initiated by the evil enemy, especially if
the soul reflects upon it and glories "in the experience of
its own sense of perception"; the transition from spiritual
to sensual pleasure here is imperceptible. For this reason,
the soul must be steeled by the withdrawal of feeling,
which can be of two kinds: withdrawal on the basis of
infidelity or as a pedagogical measure; the difference
between both experiences and the manner of behaviour
are presented in a clear and subtle way. The soul must be
taught, by an alternation of consolation and desolation,
to transfer its joy more and more from the periphery to
its innermost center—must be taught to establish itself in
'hope' which lies at a provisional point midway between
the periphery and the depths.

—Hans Urs von Balthasar

REFLECTION

Surface joy simply does not last. It is too
ephemeral, too based on emotion and like the
morning dew quickly evaporates. Centered joy,

the deep kind, is grounded in a reality far beyond the land of feelings. It is based on the experiential knowledge that one is known and loved. But the journey from the surface to the center is long and arduous. Just ask Dante. In the end, however, if one perseveres, what awaits is that peace beyond all understanding that St. Paul writes about, as well as that complete joy Jesus wished for all his disciples.

ACTION

Make a list of your five greatest joys. Are they surface or centered joys?

Discreet Joy

("But this festivity must also remain discreet, lest it insult
the immense pain of millions of women and men who
throughout the world continue to live in despair."
—Louis-Marie Chauvet)

No wet-blanket here,
just high sensitivity for those who suffer
while we enjoy—
enjoy the wine at Cana,
enjoy the sudden gift of friendship,
enjoy the surgery restoring health.

Be discreet in these festivities.
Yes, dance and sing and be merry
but, before falling asleep,
remember unto the Lord all those,
millions upon millions,
who have no wine or friends,
who live near the edge of despair.

REFLECTION

Belief in the doctrine of the Mystical Body of
Christ maintains that what one member of the
body experiences, all others do as well. Joys and
sorrows are transmitted through an incredible
mutuality. Thus, our joy is always muted, since we
are keenly aware that, at the very moment of our
joy, our brothers and sisters elsewhere on the
planet are suffering. It also means that when we
suffer, others may know the grace of joy and we

will be challenged to appreciate their good fortune. So let our festivities be discreet; let our mourning be consoled by an awareness of the empathy of others.

ACTION

Today rejoice with those who rejoice, weep with those who weep—all within the same hour.

Christian Joy: Between Tears and Laughter

*Tertullian declares that "the Christian saint is hilarious,"
hinting at the fact that to be really happy about
anything you have to be happy about everything,
and Teresa of Avila prayed to be delivered from sour,
vinegary Christians. These, however, only bring us to
the threshold of a closely related mark of this life: the
presence of Christian joy. Von Hugel took great pains
to single out this demand in the qualifications for
canonization. There must be ample evidence not only
of heroism, but of the presence of Christian joy. Yet
this joy is as mysterious and as unfathomable as the
character of sanctity itself, and like sanctity and
holiness it seems never to have been the goal, but
only the byproduct of the soul's attachment to God.*

*Joy is such an utterly different category from
pleasure or the absence of pain. It is a quivering
needle between the soul's utter satisfaction and its
contrary sense of its own bent toward nothingness,
between what Simone Weil so subtly calls Grace and
its natural countering downthrust Gravity. To "weep
for joy" is ever so natural because joy lies both between
and beyond both tears and laughter. Yet there is a great
lightening of the heart in it and a healing that knows
no equal. To a heart that has known its balm, there
can be the merriness of the scaffold itself of a Thomas
More who asks the Lord Lieutenant to help him up
the ladder with the genial "and as for the coming
down, let me shift for myself."*

—Douglas V. Steere

REFLECTION

Joy of any sort is mysterious. It is like love in that while the experience is certain, the definition and understanding are beyond us. Indeed, joy is a product of love, which means that it is taken out of the realm of pleasure or pain. A suffering person can experience joy as much as a person who is free of pain. The reason is that joy is grounded in caring, loving relationships, whatever the circumstances. As pilgrims we will be forever crying and laughing. As pilgrims we will know the possibility of joy—real as the sunlight and refreshing as a warm, spring rain.

ACTION

Be an agent of joy today by expressing your affection for someone dear to you.

DAY SEVEN
The Voice of Gladness

*Maybe that means that the voice we should listen to
most as we choose a vocation is the voice that we
might think we should listen to least, and that is the
voice of our own gladness. What can we do that makes
us gladdest, what can we do that leaves us with the
strongest sense of sailing true north and of peace, which
is much of what gladness is? Is it making things with
our own hands out of wood or stone or paint or canvas?
Or is it making something we hope for like truth out of
words? Or is it making people laugh or weep in a way
that cleanses their spirit?*

—Frederick Buechner

REFLECTION

A workshop leader once asked: "When are you happiest, most alive? You are then probably in your gifted area." Sage advice. Using gladness as an element of discernment helps us to match our talent with the needs that surround us. Whether our gift is one of craftsmanship or writing, whether it is the talent of communicating or healing, the imperative that should haunt us daily is: "Do not stay out of your gifted area too long!" If we do, it will not only be the death of us, but probably the death (of happiness) of others as well. This "following of one's bliss" need not be an individualistic, narcissistic adventure. Rather, when the discernment has been born of prayer and wise counsel, it will lead to the building up of the community.

ACTION

Think about someone you know whose gladness—because it is an expression of living one's gift—builds up the community. Get in touch with that person today, affirming his or her giftedness and expressing your gratitude for it.

WEEK SEVEN

A Heart of Praise
That I May Adore Thee!

LET IT BE WRITTEN

Why write?
Why get out pen and pad,
chain oneself to a desk,
wait on the muses,
dwell in solitude
while the rest of the world
frolics to and fro?

Prestige?
Money?
To stem the tide of time?
Why, why write?

The psalmist had a motive:
"Let this be written for ages to come
that a people yet unborn may praise the Lord" (Ps 102:18).

Adoration involves looking with love. When our hearts are full of praise, we gaze upon the Source of all life and holiness with reverence and awe. Sometimes we kneel, sometimes we sing, always we are aware of a gracious Mystery, a "God from whom all blessings flow." And when that awareness is abiding, all of life becomes a song of praise.

One gift of the Christian tradition is that communities such as the Benedictines or the Carmelites, whose central purpose is praising God, have been formed. Individuals in these communities have dedicated their lives to prayer and adoration. They remind us of transcendence; they recall for us that there is another dimension of existence that merits our loving attention. These contemplatives serve us well. They also help us to remember that the central purpose of the parish is to praise God, which is what we, as individuals, are called to do too.

An Animate Doxology

DOXOLOGY

*God fills my being to the brim
with floods of His immensity.
I drown within a drop of Him
whose sea-bed is infinity.*

*The Father's will is everywhere
for chart and chance His precept keep.
There are no beaches to His care
nor cliffs to pluck me from His deep.*

*The Son is never far away from me
for presence is what love compels.
Divinely and incarnately
He draws me where His mercy dwells.*

*And lo, myself am the abode
of Love, the third of the Triune,
the primal surge and sweep of God
and my eternal claimant soon!*

*Praise to the Father and the Son
and to the Spirit! May I be,
O Water, Wave and Tide in One,
Thine animate doxology.*

—Jessica Powers

REFLECTION

Doxology refers to praise of God. The God praised in the Christian tradition is singular in essence yet three in person: Father, Son, and

Spirit. This mystery baffles our finite comprehension. Doxology engages the heart and enables us to sing our songs of adoration even though we do not fully understand the God we honor. This should not surprise us, since we love and praise our dear ones while lacking total comprehension of who they are. When we become "animate doxologies," that is, people of living praise, we fulfill one of the most important functions of being human.

ACTION

Spend five minutes pondering: "Glory be to the Father, and to the Son, and to the Holy Spirit, as it was in the beginning, is now, and ever will be, world without end."

A Proper and Fitting Work: Praise

We should also praise God to the fullest extent of our ability. The praise of God means a person offers honor and veneration to the divine majesty throughout his life. Such praise of God is the most proper and fitting work of the angels and saints in heaven and of all loving persons on earth. A person should praise God with his heart, his desire, and his powers as these strive upward toward God; so, too, he should praise God with his words and deeds, his body and soul, and all his possessions as he uses them in humble service both exteriorly and interiorly. Those who do not praise God here on earth will remain without the power of speech in eternity. The praise of God is the most pleasant and delightful activity of a loving heart. Such a heart, full of praise itself, desires that all creatures praise God. There will be no end to this praise of God, for that is our bliss: rightly will we praise him for all eternity.

—John Ruusbroec

REFLECTION

Praise is about looking with reverence. For St. John of the Cross, contemplative prayer is essentially loving attention. When we are mindful of God with love, we are in the land of adoration, veneration—yes, praise. We leave ourselves behind and focus on the Source and Summit of our being. This activity is difficult because of our innate narcissism, our excessive preoccupation with self. It is difficult as well because our desire for action makes sitting still in silence an arduous task. Paradoxically, unless the Holy Spirit is active in the depth of our being in this form of prayer, we will not be able to "see" and thus praise our Triune God.

ACTION

When alone, sing softly all the verses of "Holy God, We Praise Thy Name." Reverently taste the theology embedded in this ancient hymn.

DAY THREE
The Ecstasy of Love

Then it can "adore." Adoration, ah! That is the word from Heaven! It seems to me it can be defined as the ecstasy of love. It is love overcome by the beauty, the strength, the immense grandeur of the Object loved, and it "falls down in a kind of faint" in an utterly profound silence, that silence of which David spoke when he exclaimed: "Silence is Your praise!"

—Elizabeth of the Trinity

REFLECTION

When a person first sees the Grand Canyon or the face of a newborn child or some incredible painting or sculpture, a sense of awe and wonder fills the soul. Sometimes the only response before such beauty is silence. We are pulled outside of self and are lost in the grandeur of the moment. If this is true in the face of various aspects of creation, what must it be like to experience, through God's gratuitous grace, a glimpse of God himself? The mystic is overcome and falls silent, thereby giving God the greatest praise possible. All "alleluias" cease, the heart is hushed, and the soul is suspended in stillness and reverent amazement.

ACTION

Take your favorite painting or song or poem and rest in its presence. Ask God to let you experience the Source of that beauty.

DAY FOUR
The Music of Eternity

So we see our Christian effectiveness is directly linked
with this adoring attention. God's Spirit is always with us.
In adoring prayer, we open our doors wide to receive it,
abase ourselves, and acknowledge our nothingness and His
wonder, perfection, and joy. The soul which has thus
given itself to God becomes part of the Mystical Body
through which He acts on life. We are destined to be
receivers and transmitters of His grace. But we are often in
such a hurry to transmit that we forget the primary need
to receive. Receiving means to keep ourselves carefully
tuned in, sensitive to the music of eternity.

—Evelyn Underhill

REFLECTION

The prayer of praise and adoration is a grace. In
this prayer we are dealing with Uncreated Grace,
that is, the self-giving of God. As recipients, we are
indebted to the Giver. Later we will be commis-
sioned to transmit what we have received, but first
we must taste fully of God's self-communication. To
the extent that we are sensitive to this divine music,
indeed, to this "silent music," we will be able to
effectively share it with others. Authentic praise and
adoration will eventually lead to communal charity.

ACTION

Spend a half hour before the Blessed Sacrament
and ask for the gift of adoration.

DAY FIVE

Let My Soul Praise Thee

Receive the sacrifice of my Confessions offered by my tongue, which Thou didst form and hast moved to confess unto Thy name. Heal Thou all my bones and they shall say: Lord, who is like Thee! A man who makes confession to Thee does not thereby give Thee any information as to what is happening within him. The closed heart does not close out Thy eye, nor the heart's hardness resist Thy hand. For Thou dost open it at Thy pleasure whether for mercy or for justice, and there is nothing that can hide itself from Thy heat. But let my soul praise Thee that it may love Thee, and let it tell Thee Thy mercies that it may praise Thee. Without ceasing Thy whole creation speaks Thy praise—the spirit of every man by the words that his mouth directs to Thee, animals and lifeless matter by the mouth of those who look upon them: that so our soul rises out of its mortal weariness unto Thee, helped upward by the things Thou hast made and passing beyond them unto Thee who hast wonderfully made them: and there refreshment is and strength unfailing.

—*St. Augustine*

REFLECTION

Confession is a prayer for forgiveness. Yet, it is also a prayer of praise, for it draws our attention to the mercy and compassion of God. St. Augustine in his *Confessions* discloses his own sinfulness. Yet, just as much, Augustine confesses the goodness, beauty, and graciousness of God. Each of these merits praise. In fact, Augustine truly believed that all creation is constantly praising God and the human person articulates that praise: As we praise and thank God, we are renewed and refreshed.

ACTION

Put *The Confessions of St. Augustine* on your reading list. Begin reading it before the end of the month.

The Three Excellences of Praise

There are three excellent qualities of the praise the soul renders God in this union. The first is that it praises Him as its duty, for it sees that God created it for His own praise, as He asserts through Isaias: This people I have formed for Myself; it will sing My praises [Is. 43:21]. The second excellence of praise is that the soul praises God for goods it receives and the delight it has in praising. The third excellence is that it praises God for what He is in Himself. Even though the soul would experience no delight, it would praise Him on account of Who He is.

—St. John of the Cross

REFLECTION

We praise God because, first of all, the very purpose of our existence is to give glory to God, which we do by being agents of God's light, love, and life. A second reason for praise is God's generosity. When we realize that everything we have and are is gift, we experience delight in praising God. Third, and most important, we offer praise simply because of the very nature of God, who is Love.

ACTION

In the morning, praise God for the mystery of creation; at noon, praise God for the gifts of family, freedom, and faith; in the evening, praise God who is Love.

DAY SEVEN

A Crown of Praise

A WREATH

A wreathed garland of deserved praise,
Of praise deserved, unto thee I give,
I give to thee, who knowest all my ways,
My crooked winding ways, wherein I live,
Wherein I die, not live: for life is straight,
Straight as a line, and ever tends to thee,
To thee, who art more far above deceit,
Than deceit seems above simplicity.
Give me simplicity, that I may live,
So live and like, that I may know thy ways,
Know them and practice them: then shall I give
For this poor wreath, give thee a crown of praise.

—*George Herbert*

REFLECTION

God deserves our praise in return for all that God has done and is doing for us. The praise expressed in flowers is symbolic. The praise that God desires is our knowing and doing the divine will. This is God's deserved praise; this is the garland of glory. What it means practically is our turning from our winding, crooked, deceitful ways and living a life of simplicity, ever tending to God.

ACTION

Begin today to construct a garland of good deeds that you might present to the Lord.

A Heart of Gratitude
That I May Thank Thee!

GETTING IN LINE

(inspired by words from a conference
given by Evelyn Underhill)

Do not get out of line
lest you get lost.
Out of line with
"the generous output of sunshine,
the uncalculated fertility of the earth,
and the great life-giving mantle of air."

So how do we stay in line,
how do we align ourselves with grace?
Generosity!

By freely giving what we have received,
without cost, without reservation,
we parallel God's liberality.

In that resides our spirituality.

Gratitude begets generosity. To appreciate and cherish
the gifts of sunshine, the good earth, and the air we
breathe is at the core not only of stewardship but also of

spirituality. God is the Giver; we are the recipients. And the gifts given are not for us alone but are to be shared with others. The danger lies in taking things for granted. The danger lies in an attitude of entitlement.

"Thank you" is a simple phrase, but when we speak it from the heart and with deep sincerity we grow in our relationship with our generous God. Radical gratitude is a transforming attitude affecting every moment and relationship. Through a life of thanksgiving we become a eucharistic people; through a life of thanksgiving we become responsible agents of the gifts given to us.

DAY ONE
Radical Gratitude

Radical gratitude begins when we stop taking life for granted. It arises in the astonishment at the miracle of creation and of our own creation. As "In the beginning," this miracle is more fundamental than anything we try to manufacture or work on. In gratitude, the vicious cycle of dissatisfaction with life is broken and we begin anew in the recognition of what we have rather than in what we don't, in the acknowledgement of who we are rather than in the awareness of who we aren't. Gratitude is the foundation of faith in God as the Creator of all beginnings, great and small. It awakens the imagination to another way of being, to another kind of economy, the great economy of grace in which each person is of infinite value and worth.

—Mary Jo Leddy

REFLECTION

Does the basic option in life come down to either radical gratitude or perpetual dissatisfaction? Why is it that for many people the glass is always half empty and all attention is focused on what is lacking rather than on enjoyment of the abundance at hand? A life of gratitude is a perpetual "thank you"—for all of creation as well as for our own existence. Radical gratitude is a whole way of living that is grounded in and colors everything with a rich sensitivity to being so blessed and so gifted. Fortunate are those children raised by parents who instilled in them a heart of gratitude.

Fortunate are those individuals who, from whatever mentor, have learned not to take a single thing for granted.

ACTION

When this day ends, before you go to sleep, count your many blessings and let the sheep number themselves.

DAY TWO
Counting Each Gift

DEO GRATIAS

I thank You, Lord, for all that You have given:
  I thank You for the mountains and the sea,
For this fair earth and Your much fairer heaven
  Which holds Your promise for eternity.
I thank You for Your lesser gifts. Oh Lord,
  Your special gifts to me,—my home, my friends—
For the health of mind and body these afford!
  I count each gift Your tender goodness sends.

But most of all I wish to thank You, God,
  For your best gifts,—for grief and bitter loss,
For hours of pain beneath Your chastening rod,
  For grace to stand alone beneath Your cross.

For what You have given and what You have denied
I thank You, Lord, at this Thanksgiving tide.

—Ruth Mary Fox

REFLECTION

The ability to say *Deo gratias* for everything is a sign of great maturity. "Good" things, like family, friends, faith, freedom, are obvious graces deserving our profound gratitude. But how many of us are able to offer thanks in the face of tragedy and suffering, pain and discomfort? The mature see these happenings (often in hindsight) as instruments of growth that would not otherwise have been possible. Acorns do not find pleasure in being buried in the dank, dark soil. Yet, unless this dying happens, there would be no oak tree—no oak tree with deep roots and outspread branches offering a silent hymn of praise in every season.

ACTION

Take a painful experience of the past and spend some time considering how that event has become for you a redemptive, not a destructive, moment.

DAY THREE
A Grateful, Chosen Heart

*I now realize, God, how much You have given me. So
much that was beautiful and so much that was hard
to bear. Yet whenever I showed myself ready to bear it,
the hard was directly transformed into the beautiful.
And the beautiful was sometimes much harder to bear,
so overpowering did it seem. To think that one small
human heart can experience so much, oh God, so much
suffering and so much love. I am so grateful to You, God,
for having chosen my heart, in these times, to experience
all the things it has experienced.*

—Etty Hillesum

REFLECTION

Etty Hillesum died in a concentration camp
before the age of thirty. Even though she endured
great suffering, she was still thankful. How opera-
tive grace was in her life. She took the hard and
painful, embraced it, and then let the grace of
God transform it into something glorious. How
mysterious and paradoxical this gratitude is.
Words fail to explain it; logic falters and fails us in
this realm of dying unto new life. Only experience
and profound acceptance have a chance of shed-
ding some light on this sacrificial process.

ACTION

Ask God to turn a painful experience/memory of
yours into something beautiful.

DAY FOUR
The Discipline of Gratitude

Gratitude, however, goes beyond the "mine" and "thine"
and claims the truth that all of life is a pure gift. In the
past I always thought of gratitude as a spontaneous
response to the awareness of gifts received, but now I
realize that gratitude can also be lived as a discipline.
The discipline of gratitude is the explicit effort to
acknowledge that all I am and have is given to me as
a gift of love, a gift to be celebrated with joy.

—*Henri J. M. Nouwen*

REFLECTION

Those individuals who have reached the status of
professionals, whether in the theater or sports or
academia, know from experience that their fluid,
"spontaneous" performance is the result of years
of discipline and hard work. While an expression
of gratitude can be a spontaneous reaction, a life of
gratitude is woven of intentionality. We are to practice a mindfulness that everything is gift and
respond accordingly. Once the discipline (let's call
it virtue) takes root, then we can live that "spontaneous" existence that gives the appearance that our
hearts are always and have forever been grateful.

ACTION

Before retiring, make a list of all the gifts that
came your way this day. Did you exercise the discipline of gratitude in giving thanks?

Everything Is a Gratuitous Gift

For our very existence, our vocation, and our redemption,
to every ray of the sun that enlivens us with its warmth
and its luster, and to every drop of water that quenches our
thirst—everything is a gratuitous gift of His inexhaustible
goodness. All the truths we are blessed in knowing, all
beauty we are allowed to enjoy; every moment of good
health and every bit of nourishment we take—all these
undeserved benefits in no wise due to us. How often do we
misuse the gifts of God; with how much ingratitude and
indifference do we requite His blessings!

—Dietrich Von Hildebrand

REFLECTION

In a culture of entitlement, gratitude is rare. It is strange how we have come to see the bounty around us as a right. It is strange how we can be so indifferent and thankless when so many blessings surround us. Misfortune sometimes awakens us to the gifts we have taken for granted. Tragedy, both personal and vicarious, gives us cause to re-examine the meaning of life and the value of all the undeserved benefits we have received. A response of gratitude means that goodness and beauty, in whatever form, will be honored, treasured, and acknowledged.

ACTION

Jot down five undeserved benefits given to you this past week.

DAY SIX
Captured by Gratitude

In a funny way, it was hard for me to get up and leave that place. Finding such a shelter on such a night had probably saved my life, and I had this feeling that I oughtn't to leave until I found somebody to thank. I felt sort of captured by gratitude.

—Wendell Berry

REFLECTION

We ought not to leave the kitchen table, the university, indeed, our beloved planet Earth without saying "Thank you!" And to whom shall we go to deliver this message of gratitude? Our moms? The institution's president? The maker of the universe? We are so deeply indebted for the many ways in which our lives have been saved. We speak here not just of our physical lives, saved from the elements, but also of our inner lives, saved from the forces of evil and corruption. Being captured by gratitude is a wonderful "enslavement." It will lead to joy and eventually peace.

ACTION

Write a note to a grade school teacher and thank that person for his or her ministry.

Owing Thanks

*Yet, Lord, I should have owed thanks to You, My God
and the most excellent Creator and Ruler of the Universe,
even if it had been Your will that I should not live
beyond boyhood. For even then I was; I lived; I felt: even
so early I had an instinct for the care of my own being,
a trace in me of that most profound Unity whence my
being was derived; in my interior sense I kept guard
over the integrity of my outward sense perception, and
in my small thoughts upon small matters I had come to
delight in the truth. I hated to be wrong, had a vigorous
memory, was well trained in speech, delighted in friendship, shunned pain, meanness and ignorance. In so small
a creature was not all this admirable and reason for
praise? Yet all these were the gifts of my God, for I did
not give them to myself. All these were good and all
these were I.*

—St. Augustine

REFLECTION

We do well not only to inventory our external possessions (in case our house catches on fire), but
also to make a thorough list of the interior gifts
that are part of our being. We do even better not
just to record them, but to reflect upon where
they came from and then express our gratitude.
St. Augustine was a master of this art. His self-
knowledge was deep and accurate; his theology
was profound and expansive. The bottom line?

All is gift and the Giver is God. Our response: eternal gratitude.

ACTION

Inventory your inner gifts. Spend some time reflecting on where those gifts came from and then open your heart to express your gratitude to the Giver.

WEEK NINE

A Heart of Kindness That I May Emulate Thee!

BEYOND ME

Almost everything is beyond me:
the inner workings of a combustion engine,
the DNA helix,
the orbiting of planets,
how gravity and grace work,
the flight of the bumblebee.

Is there anything that I truly comprehend?
Anything that is not beyond me?

One thing alone,
one thing I understand:
the kindness behind being given
a cup of water,
a word of affirmation,
a smile across a subway aisle.

The psalmist tells us that our God is kind and merciful. Made in the image and likeness of that God, we too are called to show mercy to others and to do acts of kindness for them. Whether through almsgiving, words of encouragement, heartfelt gestures of caring, or deep listening, we say to others that they are important and that they are treasured.

A telltale sign of the health of an individual or a nation is how they treat the very old and the very young, the most vulnerable in any society. As we ponder God's word, we see God's kindness toward Simeon and Anna in the temple and we see how Jesus deals with the young people whom he blesses and embraces. This is the God we are to emulate, a God who cares about all, but in a special way for those who need the most help.

We are all struggling pilgrims; we all need acts of kindness. And when kindness is received or given, the level of joy increases in both the recipient and the benefactor.

DAY ONE

The Business of Being Kind

The year 1862 was a dark spot in Henry Adams's life, and the education it gave was mostly one that he gladly forgot. As far as he was aware, he made no friends; he could hardly make enemies; yet towards the close of the year he was flattered by an invitation from Monckton Milnes to Fryston, and it was one of many acts of charity towards the young that gave Milnes immortality. Milnes made it his business to be kind. Other people criticized him for his manner of doing it, but never imitated him. Naturally, a dispirited, disheartened private secretary was exceedingly grateful, and never forgot the kindness, but it was chiefly as education that this first country visit had value.

—Henry Adams

REFLECTION

A single act of kindness can transform a life. Albert Schweitzer once wrote that a smile across the aisle can stop a suicide. We must never underestimate the power of a smile, a pat on the back, a gentle word, an invitation to belong. These acts of kindness are so affirming to those that receive them that, as in the case of Henry Adams, they are never forgotten and elicit an eternal gratitude. Making it one's business to be kind is a vocation of supreme importance.

ACTION

Reach out to a stranger with a kind word or an invitation.

A History of Kindness

It is the history of our kindnesses that alone makes this world tolerable. If it were not for that, for the effect of kind words, kind looks, kind letters...I should be inclined to think our life a practical jest in the worst possible spirit.

—Robert Louis Stevenson

REFLECTION

At times in life we are recipients; at other times in life we are benefactors. Blessed is that life in which the gifts received and given are colored by kindness. And what about a life permeated with meanness—harsh words, frowns and scowls, mean-spirited correspondence? Like a flower that is the victim of a cold snap, everything shuts down. By contrast, with warm, gracious weather, flowers open up and share their beauty with others. Such is the power and the glory of kindness. May our history of kindness, both in receiving and giving, be lengthy and well documented.

ACTION

Begin today to record acts of kindness given and received. Review that log on a monthly basis.

DAY THREE
The One Rule

Joe, a young man from Pittsburgh, came up to me with one request: "Please tell me it will all be okay."

"Welcome to Earth, young man," I said. "It's hot in the summer and cold in the winter. It's round and wet and crowded. At the outside, Joe, you've got about a hundred years here. There's only one rule that I know of: Goddamn it, Joe, you've got to be kind!"

—*Kurt Vonnegut*

REFLECTION

Is it possible in this complex world to reduce all moral living down to one inclusive imperative? Does "Be kind!" do it? Jesus would seem to demand so much more: a sacrificial love for the well-being of others. And surely this ideal should govern our deepest self. Yet, would that the world were simply kind. Here we would have a solid basis, a place from which we could then strive for so much more. The question and the request remain: Will everything, in the end, be okay? No need to wait for an answer. Our daily task is a simple one: kindness to all, including oneself.

ACTION

Think of the kindest person you know. Send that person a note of gratitude.

DAY FOUR

Kindness: The Art of Disposability

Gabriel Marcel characterizes this attitude [caring] in terms of "disposability (disponibilité), the readiness to bestow and spend oneself and make oneself available, and its contrary, indisposability." One who is disposable recognizes that she has a self to invest, to give. She does not identify herself with her objects and possessions. She is present to the cared-for. One who is indisposable, however, comes across even to one physically present as absent, as elsewhere. Marcel says: "When I am with someone who is indisposable, I am conscious of being with someone for whom I do not exist; I am thrown back on myself."

—Nel Noddings

REFLECTION

The bumper sticker that reads: "I would rather be..." says a great deal about experience of "elsewhere." It is a failure of presence; it is a failure of concern and caring; it is a failure of kindness. Kind people are disposed to the presence of others. They are not caught up in their own egos, nor is everything self-referential. Disposability, in this sense, is being available; it is the exercise of the sacrament of the moment. Kindness is impossible without the attitude of disposability.

ACTION

Refuse to multi-task. Do what you are doing. Do not practice "elsewhere."

Against the Man with the Flint

Above all, some of them [humans], a mere handful in any generation perhaps, loved—they loved the animals about them, the song of the wind, the soft voices of women. On the flat surfaces of cave walls the three dimensions of the outside world took animal shape and form. Here—not with the ax, not with the bow—man fumbled at the door of his true kingdom. Here, hidden in times of trouble behind silent brows, against the man with the flint, waited St. Francis of the birds—the lovers, the men who are still forced to walk warily among their kind.

—Loren Eiseley

REFLECTION

How many kind, loving human beings live in any given generation? How many are there who travel with ax, bow, and flint? Humans tend to be aggressive, domineering, and self-centered creatures. To encounter a St. Francis or a Good Samaritan is truly a grace. And to be one of them—ah, the working of grace. Let us love animals and flowers; let us hear the song and music of the wind and stars; let us be silent before the voices of those who speak of love and wisdom. Then kindness will sweep across the land and fill our hearts with joy.

ACTION

Take a walk and listen to the song of the wind, the hymn of the birds.

A Compassionate Doer

He was by nature a compassionate doer of kind deeds whereas my own nature has always been—through diffidence and a sense of inadequacy as much as anything—to look the other way in the face of human need, so that such kindnesses as I have done in my life I have usually either had to force myself to do, or been forced by someone else, or have thought of as so alien to my nature that I have never been able very satisfactorily to take credit for them.

—Frederick Buechner

REFLECTION

Temperament is important. Each of us has a certain "nature" that colors our days and our actions. Compassionate people, "by nature," have a deep sense of the plight of others and reach out to the suffering. Those who are more reserved, "by nature," tend to hold back and avoid involvement. Thus, the importance of the training of one's moral character. Despite our innate dispositions, we can, by grace and effort, "force" ourselves to act with kindness and compassion. Acting *contra naturam* (contrary to nature) can often be the working of grace.

ACTION

Face some human need today and respond with kindness.

More Than Kind Words

("*You get more done with a kind word and a gun
than with a kind word alone.*"
—*Al Capone*)

Does God tote a gun?
One would think not,
this God who speaks tenderly to his people,
who is called Love,
who is known as Mercy.

Yet, David felt the bullets of accusation
via Nathan, God's prophet.
Even Peter's heart was riddled with buckshot
as Jesus glanced across the evening fire of betrayal.
And was not the sword
that pierced Mary's heart
somehow part of a divine design?

I sit here in (apparent) safety,
pondering whether or not God has an arsenal
beside his lexicon of kind words.

REFLECTION

It is possible—just ask any grandparent—to kill
with kindness. There is a need for disciplinary language, just as there is for a gentle, soft vocabulary.
The trick lies in knowing what words to use and
when and in what tone. Words spoken in an
atmosphere of violence (while toting a gun) will
eventually backfire. Words spoken with firmness

and out of love will bring healing. One suspects that Al Capone was not raised with kind words and thus he reverted to guns to deliver his message. What a tragedy for him and for all those who crossed his path.

ACTION

As you go through this day, pay close attention to the words you speak and to the tone of voice you use.

WEEK TEN

A Heart of Hospitality That I May Welcome Thee!

*("the sweet small clumsy feet of April came
into the ragged meadow of my soul."
—e. e. cummings)*

March has amazing hands,
stirring the air into volatile winds.
And May has a gentle, affectionate heart,
affirming the shy flowers to unfold their beauty.
But April—
ah, feet—"sweet small clumsy"—
and stepping into the inner sanctuary of our lives.

Welcome all.
Our spiritual meadows need
cleansing winds,
loving affection,
time's life-giving visitations.

This leaves three quarters of the year—
from June to February,
to work their magic.
Gratitude for their gifts
must await another prayerful verse.

For most of us, hospitality is selective, not universal. Like the child finding and separating out the unwanted peas hidden in the casserole, we exclude those things we find distasteful. For some it is the rejection of the blizzards of January; for others, the exclusion of individuals based on race or creed. Our hospitality constantly needs expansion.

My home town was once called "Welcome." I am not sure if the townspeople lived up to its name, but the ideal set forth is worthy of embracing. To be a welcoming community, truly sharing and caring, especially in relation to the stranger, is to have a heart similar to that of Christ Jesus. His glance and his tone of voice said: "You are at home with me."

DAY ONE

Welcoming the Divine Guest

The Soul that hath a Guest
Doth seldom go abroad—
Diviner Crowd at Home—
Obliterate the need—

And Courtesy forbid
A Host's departure when
Upon Himself be visiting
The Emperor of Men—

—Emily Dickinson

REFLECTION

What do we find when we gaze within? If there
indwells a divine guest—more, a divine crowd—
then extensive travel abroad seems unnecessary
and inappropriate. Basic human courtesy demands that we remain at home offering hospitality to the Emperor of humanity. If, on the other
hand, there is no one home or no one to offer
lodging to, travel abroad year after year seems fitting. We could do worse.

The monk Thomas Merton maintained that the
true journey was interior. To venture into the
depths of the soul wherein Divinity awaits is one of
our central human tasks. Yet we hesitate, fearful
that perhaps there is nothing or no one there.
Instead of looking deep within, we may turn to
activism, hoping to distract ourselves from our

fundamental loneliness. What we really need is the gift of faith, which assures us that we have been (and continue to be) visited by no one less than our Triune God.

ACTION

Upon arising in the morning and retiring at night, pause for a full minute to acknowledge the presence of the Divine Guest within.

DAY TWO
A Kind Welcoming

So I came to Milan, to the bishop and devout servant of God, Ambrose, famed among the best men of the whole world, whose eloquence did then most powerfully minister to Thy people the fatness of Thy wheat and the joy of Thy oil and the sober intoxication of Thy wine. All unknowing I was brought by God to him, that knowing I should be brought by him to God. That man of God received me as a father, and as bishop welcomed my coming. I came to love him, not at first as a teacher of the truth, which I had utterly despaired of finding in Your church, but for his kindness towards me.

—St. Augustine

REFLECTION

God's timing and providence are exquisite. Little do we know the divine design as people welcome us into their hearts and their homes. All that gracious hospitality is the operation of grace, hidden from us in the present but clearly recognized in hindsight. What would Augustine's life have been had not Ambrose greeted him with kindness and affection? Hospitality of this nature is transformative; hospitality of this kind calls for eternal gratitude.

ACTION

Send a note today to a person who offered you hospitality at a key moment in your life.

DAY THREE
Making Room

*The celebrating community can bring itself alive when all
the members of the community acknowledge a direct and primary responsibility of hospitality to one another. Hospitality
best translates the meaning of Christian community love.
Hospitality is a form of caring enough for others to give
them space in your life and to welcome them in. Hospitality
says: "There is room right now for you in my life and I want
to make it clear to you right now that there is room, and I
am hoping that there is room right now in your life for me."
Hospitality is precise and careful in its demands. It does
not seek any long-term friendship or lasting relationships. It
asks for presence and attention from each member of the
community for the duration of the celebration.*

—*Eugene Walsh, SS*

REFLECTION

What a gift it is to be given presence and attention.
What a grace it is to offer others room in our
minds and hearts. Given the nature of the human
journey—this long, lonely pilgrimage—the gift of
welcome cannot be overestimated. For however
brief a time, we receive from or we offer to another
a sense of belonging, a sense of being cared about.

ACTION

Greet two strangers today and be truly present to
them.

A Delicate Hospitality

For to the Fathers of the Desert hospitality was a duty that ranked higher than almost any other, and when a stranger came to a hermit's door, the holy man would ply him with the best food at his command, and, in the true spirit of delicate hospitality, break his fast and eat with him. Did a heart-broken sinner, scorned by the world and cast out by the church, seek compassion and tender human sympathy? It was to the solitaries that he turned in his bitter hour, for these austere and silent men had discovered the secret of Christ's love for the outcast, in an age when the church had already forgotten it. Did famine or pestilence scourge the cities? It was to the men of the desert they sent to tend the sick, organize collections, and superintend the distribution of food.

—Brigid E. Herman

REFLECTION

Hospitality is active in every form of love. Whatever the other's need, the hospitable heart responds in an appropriate and generous fashion. We can learn from the desert fathers. When the stranger or the sinner, the lonely or the lost appear at the door of our heart, there is but one rule: We must drop whatever we are doing and turn our attention and affection to that individual.

ACTION

Visit a nursing home this week and offer a resident your compassion, your kindness, your hospitality.

The Unknown God

I knew that no matter what door you knock on in a Cretan village, it will be opened for you. A meal will be served in your honor and you will sleep between the best sheets in the house. In Crete the stranger is still the unknown god. Before him all doors and all hearts are opened.

—*Nikos Kazantzakis*

REFLECTION

One person defined culture "as the way they do things around here." In Crete they do something glorious when a stranger approaches. He or she is given the royal treatment. A warm welcome, a good meal, comfortable sleeping quarters, an open heart! Is there any better description of hospitality in its concreteness? Would that the world would treat strangers in this fashion; would that the world were hospitable.

ACTION

Reflect on how you have treated strangers in the past month or so.

DAY SIX
Hospitality and Responsibility

And he [the little prince] went back to meet the fox.
"Goodbye," he said.

"Goodbye," said the fox. "And now here is my secret, a
very simple secret: It is only with the heart that one can
see rightly; what is essential is invisible to the eye."

"What is essential is invisible to the eye," the little
prince repeated so that he would be sure to remember.

"It is the time you have wasted for your rose that
makes your rose so important."

"It is the time I have wasted for my rose—" said the
little prince, so that he would be sure to remember.

"Men have forgotten this truth," said the fox. "But
you must not forget it. You become responsible, forever,
for what you have tamed. You are responsible for your
rose…"

"I am responsible for my rose," the little prince
repeated, so that he would be sure to remember.

—Antoine de Saint-Exupéry

REFLECTION

There are different levels of hospitality. The
more superficial kind involves minimal responsibility. For example, we welcome into our heart a
stranger passing by for just a day. But there is a
deeper hospitality and a more demanding
responsibility. When we welcome into our garden
a rose plant, we are getting serious. Fertilization,
watering, and protection become duties. These
are all intrinsic in the greeting and welcoming.

And when that rose is a person—be it a child, a friend, or a colleague—then our duties increase. Hospitality and responsibility have a mutual relationship and require discernment.

ACTION

Take some time to assess what your hospitality is responsible for.

A Poverty-Stricken Dwelling

*We must not become upset and worried by the
humiliations which come from the aspect we present
to the world. Let us shelter behind this outer husk
and enjoy God, who is all in all to us. Let us benefit
by our weaknesses and failures, our fears and doubts;
let us draw good from our infirmities, which make us
need special food and care, and from the contempt we
are shown. Let us find all our happiness in God, who
by these means gives himself to us as our only good. He
wants the dwelling we offer him to be poverty-stricken
and without any of those manifestations of holiness
which win such admiration for other souls.*

—*Jean-Pierre De Caussade*

REFLECTION

The first beatitude ("Blessed are the poor in
spirit") is essentially about hospitality. Those who
are poor in spirit are empty within, thus creating
space for God. To the extent that we are filled
either with things or even "virtues," our souls
become crowded with stuff and perhaps even with
self-righteousness. Or, when we are humiliated or
struggling with various sins and failures, we
become preoccupied, and the "no vacancy" sign
has to be turned on. The Lord knocks, but the
noise and din inside keep us from hearing; our
preoccupations prevent us from being aware of
the Lord's presence—much less opening the

door. The grace of a "poverty-stricken dwelling" appears to be a strange but happy blessing.

ACTION

Set aside time to do some housekeeping today. After conducting an inner inventory of the things that fill your soul, discard one attitude that blocks the Lord's entrance.

WEEK ELEVEN

A Heart of Hope
That I May Trust in Thee!

HOPE

("...the art of wise forgetting."
—Evelyn Underhill)

Is there wisdom in forgetting,
forgetting the trivial,
the superfluous,
the inane?

Like the missed free throw in the championship game,
or the blunder in the graduation talk,
or the planting of the tulips upside down?
These memories foster self-absorption,
blind us to the present,
waste tons of energy.

To be an artist of wise forgetting
is to become an agent of hope.

There is a tension, sometimes healthy, sometimes not, in
our dealing with time: the past, the present, the future. To
forget totally is to lose any sense of identity; to grasp the past
as if it were everything is just as dangerous. To experience

the sacrament of the moment is a grace, yet we are also aware of the "tyranny of the immediate." And as for the future, while glancing ahead we must not let possible worries and anxieties consume the soul.

Hope becomes possible to the extent that we foster the art of wise forgetting and the skill of keeping the present moment in perspective. It comes down to a radical trust, a confidence that God's promise of presence is real. If we believe that we step through the future into Eternity, into the fullness of God's light and love, then we will be agents of hope for a world weary and worn.

The Exercise of Hope

Sophia saved the Ashley family through the exercise of hope. "Saved" was her brother's and sisters' word for what she accomplished. She had had a long experience of hope. Hope (deep-grounded hope, not those sporadic cries and promptings wrung from us in extremity that more resemble despair) is a climate of mind and an organ of apprehension. Later we shall consider its relation to faith in the life of Sophia's father, who was a man of faith, though he did not know that he was man of faith....It is doubtful whether hope—or any of the other manifestations of creativity—can sustain itself without an impulse injected by love. So absurd and indefensible is hope. Sophia's was nourished by love of her mother and sisters, but above all by love of those two distant outcasts, her father and her brother.

—Thornton Wilder

REFLECTION

Hope is elusive yet so real. As a climate and atmosphere of the mind, it refuses to yield to skepticism, that somber cloud always hiding the sun. As an organ of apprehension, hope opens the soul to fresh possibilities. Since hope is the virtue of the "not-yet," it relies on faith in times of doubt and always on love when the journey is lonely. Sustained by these graces, hope has the possibility of "saving" us. What we need is that "deep-grounded hope," that power to be steadfast and patient though our dreams and values are threatened.

ACTION

Reflect on your own history. At what times in your life has hope opened your soul to fresh possibilities? Name two people who have been agents of hope to you.

Hope in the Face of Disaster

Whatever actually happens, precisely as such, has to be regarded as the act of God, whatever other comments on it we may wish to make. If this is taken seriously, it is impossible to regard anything at all that happens in this world as simply disastrous. Disaster is always disaster relative to some particular hope or desire; no disaster within our life in this world can be, simply, disaster from the point of view of eternal life and bliss. On the other hand, no success within this world can be regarded as simply success from the point of view of eternal life, because it always remains possible that we shall bungle our death. But this sobering reflection needs to be kept in proper perspective. God's purpose is our salvation; we should not think of him maliciously trying to catch us out, waiting, as it were, to catch us off guard and pounce on us when we are in sin. All his works are for the making of man, not for his undoing. And so it is more fundamental to a truly theological view of life to be hopeful than to be anxious. Even things that go wrong are within the overall process whereby God leads us to himself. After all, the epitome of all sin and all disaster, the murder of the Son of God, is the very centre of all hope. That is the way in which God takes our sin and our suffering into account, and that is how we, too, must take it into account.

—*Simon Tugwell*

REFLECTION

Interpreting what happens in life is a most difficult and, at times, dangerous task. This is certainly true when dealing with disasters of nature that wipe out thousands of lives. It is even more true in the face of the Holocaust and other horrendous crimes committed by human beings against other human beings. At times it is best to remain silent in the face of mystery. Yet, in faith and hope, we can make certain claims: God does will our salvation; God's works are not for our "undoing." Again, in faith and hope, we kneel before the crucifix wherein we seek the center of our hope. Beyond this, let us, even the theologians, be still.

ACTION

Spend twenty minutes on your knees before the crucifix.

"A Passion for the Possible"

*Such persons [who have a "passion for the possible"] live
their freedom in the light of hope. In spite of the darkness
of sin, despair, inhumanity and persecution, they experience the "how much more" of God's promise of redemption.
To live in freedom (and hence to live the Beatitudes)
means to assess the formative potential in such seemingly
negative experiences as suffering and death. Despite the
negativity of the Cross, the disciples are free to hope in
the face of what appears to be impossible. Their passion
for the possible enables them to validate the Resurrection.
By living in the light of hope, they are able to glimpse
the fullness of peace and joy awaiting them.*

—Susan Muto

REFLECTION

Luke's gospel tells us that nothing is impossible for
God. When we believe this, when we have a passion
for the possible, our days are different. Rather than
laboring under the burden of anxiety and fear, we
lean into our existence with an expectancy based
upon hope, knowing that, no matter what happens,
God is with and for us. In this is our joy and peace,
despite what the world might dish out to us and
despite the realities of suffering and death.

ACTION

Draw up a list of your hopes, large and small.

The Keynote of Hope

No fact in human nature is more characteristic than its
willingness to live on a chance. The existence of the
chance makes the difference, as Edmund Gurney says,
between a life of which the keynote is resignation and a
life in which the keynote is hope.

—William James

REFLECTION

There is a great continental divide in the soul. On
one side is that life of resignation that is unable to
move into the future with a sense of freshness and
new possibilities. The future is a dead-end alley. On
the other side is the ability to see in the acorn an oak
tree, in the caterpillar a butterfly. It is a vision not
limited by empiricism. It is a reality rich in potential
and accompanied by a vibrant enthusiasm.

ACTION

Find and keep an acorn in your pocket/purse.

Promises, Commitment, and Hope

Philosopher Hannah Arendt captures the importance of this capacity when she says, "The remedy for unpredictability, for the chaotic uncertainty of the future, is contained in the faculty to make and keep promises." Commitments rescue life from being a series of random encounters interrupting our isolation. We link our lives to people and to values in the hope that we may learn to be fruitful in consistent ways.

—Evelyn Eaton and James D. Whitehead

REFLECTION

Promise-making is integral to a truly human way of life. We rely on the words of others—words of a marriage promise, words in an oral contract, words of direction, whether geographic or spiritual. With our limited knowledge and insight, we depend upon the wisdom of the past and the counsel of the present. Without promises, our future is unmoored and completely unpredictable. With promises, we have an anchor in hope.

ACTION

Write out in a journal the promises you have made to yourself.

"A Feathered Hope"

> *"Hope" is the thing with feathers—*
> *That perches in the soul—*
> *And sings the tune without the words—*
> *And never stops—at all—*
>
> *And sweetest—in the Gale—is heard—*
> *And sore must be the storm—*
> *That could abash the little Bird*
> *That kept so many warm—*
>
> *I've heard it in the chillest land—*
> *And on the strangest Sea—*
> *Yet, never in Extremity,*
> *It asked a crumb—of Me.*
>
> *—Emily Dickinson*

REFLECTION

The above "job description" of hope includes many activities. Hope perches, sings, warms, and asks for nothing in return. Hope is a subtle presence that gives us confidence in the future. Hope is a songster whose melody offers strength and courage. Hope ventures into the margins of existence to do her work. Hope is sheer grace, offered to anyone who is willing to believe in promises, to live on expectations.

ACTION

Today, make someone a promise that affords that person a sense of hope.

"Something Inside"

A man is more, much more, than bone and blood and meat. Blood and meat we treat alike when we fight in battle, and we give our orders to them and every man is as useful or not as his neighbor. But when he is hurt or dying or recovering, or longing for whatever it is he longs for, then—then there is something inside him that shows, in ways you cannot put your finger on, and it is the most true thing about him, and the most important.

—*Paul Horgan*

REFLECTION

Could it be that our longings, desires, and hopes are the most important things inside each of us? Though they many be hard to name, these deep inner realities guide and motivate our days. Often it is in times of crisis and tragedy that we are awakened to them, since our ordinary days and daily distractions keep them buried. The "grace" of hurt and death, of trial and challenge, may be the necessary means of their discovery. Once they are found, life is totally different.

ACTION

Ask someone today what his or her deepest longing is.

REFERENCES CITED

PREFACE

The New American Bible, St. Joseph Edition (New York: Catholic Publishing Co., 1970).

Dag Hammarskjold, *Markings*, translated by Leif Sjoberg and W. H. Auden (New York: Alfred A. Knopf, 1981), p. 100.

WEEK ONE

DAY 1   Henry David Thoreau, *Walden; or, Life in the Woods* (New York: Signet Classic, 1960), pp. 149–50.

DAY 2   Mohandas K. Gandhi, *Autobiography: The Story of My Experiments with Truth,* translated by Mahadev Desai (New York: Dover Publications, Inc., 1948), p. 454.

DAY 3   Dag Hammarskjold, *Markings*, translated by Leif Sjoberg and W. H. Auden (New York: Alfred A. Knopf, 1981), pp. 109, 103.

DAY 4   *Meister Eckhart*, trans. Raymond Blakney (New York: Harper & Row, Publishers, 1941), p. 185.

DAY 5   Mohandas K. Gandhi, *Autobiography: The Story of My Experiments with Truth,* translated by Mahadev Desai (New York: Dover Publications, Inc., 1948), p. 294.

DAY 6   Ronald Rolheiser, *Seeking Spirituality: Guidelines for a Christian Spirituality for the Twenty-First Century* (London: Hodder & Stoughton, 1998), p. 191.

DAY 7   Romano Guardini, *The Lord* (Chicago: Henry Regnery Company, 1954), p. 490.

WEEK TWO

DAY 1   Brigid E. Herman, *Creative Prayer* (Brewster, MA: Paraclete Press, 1998), pp. 9–10.

DAY 2   Romano Guardini, *The Lord* (Chicago: Charles Regnery Company, 1954), p. 268.

DAY 3   *The Cloud of Unknowing*, trans. James Walsh, SJ (New York: Paulist Press, 1981), p. 148.

DAY 4   Ladislaus Boros, *Open Spirit* (New York: Paulist Press, 1974), p. 149.

DAY 5   Lewis Thomas, *Late Night Thoughts on Listening to Mahler's Ninth Symphony* (New York: Viking, 1983), p. 43.

DAY 6   Joseph Gallagher, *How to Survive Being Human* (Westminster, MD: Christian Classics, 1970), p. 67.

DAY 7   Raissa Maritain, *Raissa's Journal*, presented by Jacques Maritain (Albany, NY: Magi Books, Inc., 1963), p. 115.

WEEK THREE

DAY 1   Peter van Breeman, SJ, *The God Who Won't Let Go* (Notre Dame, IN: Ave Maria Press, 2001), p. 25.

DAY 2   Viktor E. Frankl, *Man's Search for Meaning* (New York: Washington Square Press, 1946), p. 57.

DAY 3   Karl Rahner, *On Prayer* (Collegeville, MN: The Liturgical Press, 1958), p. 92.

DAY 4   Pope Paul VI (Cardinal Montini), quoted by Peter Hebblethwaite in *Paul VI: The First Modern Pope* (New York: Paulist Press, 1993), pp. 273–74.

DAY 5   Gerald Vann, *St. Thomas Aquinas* (Chicago: Benzinger Brothers, 1940), pp. 25–26.

DAY 6   Samuel Taylor Coleridge, "The Rime of the Ancient Mariner," *The New Oxford Book of English Verse 1250–1950*, chosen and edited by Helen Gardner (New York: Oxford University Press, 1972), p. 544.

DAY 7   *The Collected Works of St. John of the Cross,* translated by Kieran
         Kavanaugh, OCD, and Otilio Rodriguez, OCD (Washington,
         DC: ICS Publications, Institute of Carmelite Studies, 1973),
         p. 517.

WEEK FOUR

DAY 1   Teilhard de Chardin, *The Divine Milieu* (New York: Harper
         Torchbooks, 1960), p. 135.

DAY 2   Rowan Williams, *The Wound of Knowledge* (Boston: Cowley,
         1979), p. 89.

DAY 3   Romano Guardini, *The Life of Faith,* translated by John Chapin
         (Westminster, MD: The Newman Press, 1960), p. 96.

DAY 4   Avery Dulles, SJ, *The Assurance of Things Hoped For* (New York:
         Oxford University Press, 1994), p. 279.

DAY 5   Alan Paton, *For You Departed* (New York: Charles Scribner's
         Sons, 1969), p. 17.

DAY 6   Alec Guinness, *Blessings in Disguise* (New York: Alfred A.
         Knopf, 1984), pp. 42–43.

DAY 7   Ernest Becker, *The Denial of Death* (New York: The Free Press,
         1973), pp. 257–58.

WEEK FIVE

DAY 1   Whittaker Chambers, *Witness* (New York: Random House,
         1952), p. 113.

         C. S. Lewis, *Surprised by Joy* (New York: Harcourt, Brace &
         World, Inc., 1955), p. 161.

DAY 2   Harper Lee, *To Kill a Mockingbird* (Philadelphia: J. B.
         Lippincott, 1960), p. 116.

DAY 3   Ladislaus Boros, *Open Spirit* (New York: Paulist Press, 1974), p. 35.

DAY 4   Evelyn Underhill, *The Ways of the Spirit* (New York: Crossroad,
         1993), p. 160.

DAY 5   From an address given by Alexander Solzhenitsyn at Harvard
        Class Day, Afternoon Exercises, Thursday, June 8, 1978.

DAY 6   Song from the 1939 film *The Wizard of Oz,* with lyrics by E. Y.
        Harburg.

DAY 7   M. Scott Peck, *The Road Less Traveled* (New York: Touchstone
        Books, 1978), p. 131.

WEEK SIX

DAY 1   Philip D. Kenneson, *Life on the Vine: Cultivating the Fruit of the
        Spirit in Christian Community* (Downers Grove, IL: Intervarsity
        Press, 1999), p. 58.

DAY 2   Robert McAfee Brown, *Creative Dislocation—The Movement of
        Grace* (Nashville: Abingdon, 1980), p. 96.

DAY 3   Susan Muto, *Blessings That Make Us Be: Living the Beatitudes*
        (New York: Crossroad, 1982), p. 81.

DAY 4   Hans Urs von Balthasar, *The Glory of the Lord: A Theological
        Aesthetics, Volume 1: Seeing the Form* (San Francisco: Ignatius
        Press, 1982) pp. 280–81.

DAY 6   Douglas V. Steere, *Together in Solitude* (New York: Crossroad,
        1982), pp. 195–96.

DAY 7   Frederick Buechner, *The Hungering Dark* (New York: The
        Seabury Press, 1981), pp. 31–32.

WEEK SEVEN

DAY 1   *The Selected Poetry of Jessica Powers,* edited by Regina Siegfried,
        ASC, and Robert F. Morneau (Washington, DC: ICS
        Publications, 1999), p. 191.

DAY 2   John Ruusbroec, *The Spiritual Espousals and Other Works* (New
        York: Paulist Press, 1985), p. 80.

DAY 3   Elizabeth of the Trinity, *The Complete Works: Volume One,* trans-
        lated by Sister Aletheia Kane, OCD (Washington, DC: ICS
        Publications, 1984), p. 150.

DAY 4   Evelyn Underhill, *The Ways of the Spirit* (New York: Crossroad, 1993), p. 176.

DAY 5   *The Confessions of St. Augustine*, translated by F. J. Sheed (New York: Sheed & Ward, 1943), p. 83.

DAY 6   *The Collected Works of St. John of the Cross*, translated by Kieran Kavanaugh, OCD, and Otilio Rodriguez, OCD (Washinton, DC: ICS Publications, Institute of Carmelite Studies, 1973), p. 643.

DAY 7   George Herbert, *The Country Parson, The Temple*, edited and with an introduction by John N. Wall, Jr. (New York: Paulist Press, 1981), p. 313.

WEEK EIGHT

DAY 1   Mary Jo Leddy, *Radical Gratitude* (Maryknoll, NY: Orbis Books, 2002), p. 7.

DAY 2   Ruth Mary Fox, *Some Did Return* (Fort Lauderdale, FL: Wakebrooks House, 1976), p. 86.

DAY 3   *An Interrupted Life: The Diaries of Etty Hillesum 1941–1943* (New York: Washington Square Press, 1981), p. 207.

DAY 4   Henri J. M. Nouwen, *The Return of the Prodigal Son* (New York: Doubleday, Image Books, 1992), p. 85.

DAY 5   Dietrich Von Hildebrand, *Transformation in Christ: On the Christian Attitude* (San Francisco: Ignatius Press, 1940), pp. 293–94.

DAY 6   Wendell Berry, *Jayber Crow* (Washington, DC: Counterpoint Press, 2000), p. 83.

DAY 7   *The Confessions of St. Augustine*, translated by F. J. Sheed (New York: Sheed & Ward, 1943), p. 23.

WEEK NINE

DAY 1   Henry Adams, *The Education of Henry Adams*, with an introduction by Edmund Morris (New York: The Modern Library, 1999), pp. 137–38.

DAY 2 Robert Louis Stevenson, source unknown; quoted by Kay Redfield Jamison in *An Unquiet Mind: A Memoir of Moods and Madness* (New York: Viking, 1995), p. 146.

DAY 3 Kurt Vonnegut, *A Man without a Country* (New York: Random House Trade Paperbacks, 2005), p. 107.

DAY 4 Nel Noddings, *Caring: A Feminine Approach to Ethics and Moral Education* (Berkeley: University of California Press, 1984), p. 19.

DAY 5 Loren Eiseley, *The Unexpected Universe* (New York: A Harvest Book, Harcourt Brace Jovanovich, Inc., 1964), p. 188.

DAY 6 Frederick Buechner, *The Sacred Journey* (San Francisco: Harper & Row, Publishers, 1982), p. 94.

WEEK TEN

DAY 1 *The Complete Poems of Emily Dickinson*, edited by Thomas H. Johnson (Boston: Little, Brown and Company, 1960), #674, p. 335.

DAY 2 *The Confessions of St. Augustine*, translated by F. J. Sheed (New York: Sheed & Ward, 1943), p. 100.

DAY 3 Eugene Walsh, SS, *Practical Suggestions for Celebrating Sunday Mass* (Glendale, AZ: Pastoral Arts Associates of North America, 1978), p. 30.

DAY 4 Brigid E. Herman, *Creative Prayer* (Brewster, MA: Paraclete Press, 1998), p. 27.

DAY 5 Nikos Kazantzakis, *Report to Greco*, translated by P. A. Bien (New York: Simon and Schuster, 1961), p. 312.

DAY 6 Antoine de Saint-Exupéry, *The Little Prince* (Reynal & Hitchcock, 1943), pp. 87–88.

DAY 7 Jean-Pierre De Caussade, *Abandonment to Divine Providence* (New York: Image Books, 1975), p. 91.

WEEK ELEVEN

DAY 1 Thornton Wilder, *The Eighth Day* (New York: Harper & Row, Publishers, 1967), p. 57.

DAY 2   Simon Tugwell, *The Beatitudes: Soundings in Christian Traditions* (Springfield, IL: Templegate Publishers, 1980), p. 39.

DAY 3   Susan Muto, *Blessings that Make Us Be: A Formative Approach to Living the Beatitudes* (New York: Crossroad, 1987), p. 5.

DAY 4   William James, *The Varieties of Religious Experience: A Study of Human Nature* (New York: The Modern Library, 1902), p. 516.

DAY 5   Evelyn Eaton and James D. Whitehead, *A Sense of Sexuality* (New York: Doubleday, 1989), p. 61.

DAY 6   *The Complete Poems of Emily Dickinson*, edited by Thomas H. Johnson (Boston: Little, Brown and Company, 1960), #254, p. 116.

DAY 7   Paul Horgan, *A Distant Trumpet* (New York: Farrar, Straus & Giroux, 1965), p. 225.